The Many Faces of Posttraumatic Stress Disorder

Susan Rau Stocker

Independent Marriage and
Family Therapist

D1449277

Holy Macro! Books

Box 82, Uniontown, OH 44685

The Many Faces of PTSD

© 2010 Susan Stocker

Written by: Susan Rau Stocker

Editors: Alice J. MacDonald, Malvina T. Rau

Design & Layout: Fine Grains (India) Private Limited, New Delhi, India.

Cover Design: Bob D'Amico

Published by: Holy Macro! Books, Box 82, Uniontown OH 44685, USA

Distributed by: Independent Publishers Group

First Printing: June 2010. Printed in USA

ISBN: 978-1-61547-002-0

Library of Congress Control Number: 2010904991

Contents

Introduction

In twenty years as a marriage and family therapist, I have learned a great deal about Posttraumatic Stress Disorder, hereafter PTSD. I have learned every bit of it *involuntarily*, by working with survivors who had themselves *involuntarily* become victims. No one volunteers for PTSD.

This book is organized around case studies and client profiles. All of the profiles have been fictionalized, as I have combined various stories and changed all identifying details.

From these courageous people, I have garnered what it means to have survived a trauma which, by definition for PTSD, is a trauma outside the normal realm of everyday life--with all of <u>its</u> inherent wounds and pain. As clients have shared with me their heartaches, their hang-ups, their suffering, their sadness, their depression, their anxiety, their weakness and their indomitable strength, I have pieced together, from many faces, the picture of the trauma survivor.

This book is my attempt to share with each of you what has been given so generously to me as clients have allowed me to learn with them and from them and because of them. One of the best ways to get through a trauma is to find meaning in the trauma. This is what Betty Rollins did with her cancer experience when she wrote <u>First, You Cry.</u> Viktor Frankel also wrote <u>Man's Search for Meaning</u> at least in part to find empathy for himself and others and to help us learn from his traumatic experiences at Auschwitz.

Let me introduce you to PTSD in much the same way I was introduced to it: one story at a time. I think you, too, will come to see the many faces of PTSD. It is my hope that you will come to understand and appreciate with great compassion the multiple effects, often lifelong, of trauma, whether it be your own trauma or the trauma of another.

One important, irrefutable caution: I attended a weeklong workshop run by Elizabeth Kubler Ross. It was a workshop on death and dying, and at least half the participants were terminally ill. The rest of us were those working with the dying. One of her resounding messages, as each of us tried to minimize our own grief, was that "it doesn't matter if the elephant is standing on your little toe or your whole foot." In other words: DO NOT compare your pain or your trauma to that of anyone else. Trauma is trauma. Honor it.

After the stress of trauma a number of resultant devastations litter the psyches and behaviors of survivors, like the branches and debris on the ground after a storm. The smaller the storm, the smaller the amount of fallout. The greater the storm, the greater the number of casualties, including the wounded and the dead, whether literally or metaphorically.

Let me also say how important it is that the psychic house one has built be strong. Biblically, the prescription is to build our houses on rock, not sand. Obviously, a child has only a sandcastle, a structure easily destroyed in the slightest of storms. And, indeed, it is the rare adult whose psychic house is so firmly constructed that the house can withstand trauma.

Our psychic houses are a multi-generational construct. Their foundations are a legacy from our grandparents and parents of good discipline, security, joy, encouragement, sound boundaries, strong values, reasonable beliefs.

Our culture and societal group decides what the houses look like, how they present themselves to the world. To use some popular stereotypes: is this house going to be a fanatically clean, hard-working Germanic home or a sprawling, colorful, easy-going hacienda? Then we furnish it with what's important to us: books, music, the latest technology, beautiful clothes and jewels, children, pets, fancy furniture or comfy stuff, food from gardens. You get the idea. Then we go about either welcoming people in or keeping them out. Those lucky enough to have been gifted and prodded to create strong houses will be much more likely to come through a trauma psychically intact. Soldiers, for example, who went to war with no previous traumas in their lives, had a template against which to contrast the irrationality and insanity of war.

Enough introduction. Still, that's more than I had before I met Brenda.

■

Brenda

Her Story

She came into the Victim Assistance office early one morning with a four year old in tow. She had gotten the older child to school and somehow found her way to us. When she and the child came into my office, and we shut the door, she started sobbing uncontrollably.

She was a battered and abused wife, and she looked the part. Her thin face was without color, her blondish hair without style, her clothes without form. The child looked terrified. He buried his head in his mother's lap and cried along. I felt like crying, too.

Her fear was for the boys, especially the one in fourth grade whom her husband had recently started to abuse. She could take it; she even thought she herself deserved it. After all, he did everything. The translation of "everything" turned out to be that he provided all the money. She couldn't even get the house straightened up or get a good meal on the table.

I was as new to the business of being a therapist as she was to the business of being a client. We muddled along together as her story told itself. She was not a woman you could warm up to. She was devoid of the social niceties: no manners, no appreciation, no interest in anyone other than herself and her children. In fact, she felt to me like a bottomless pit. What could ever be enough to fill this woman's heart and give her some hope?

Within six weeks I thought we were doing extraordinarily well. She was out of the house and living in a battered women's shelter. She had gotten a haircut, some clothes that fit, and she reported that her school-aged child was happy at the shelter. The four year old looked like he had gained some weight. He had some color in his cheeks as well as a little bag of toys he carried with him now. Brenda was enrolled in a program to retrain housewives. When she finished that program, they would help her find an apartment and a job. Legal aid would enable her to sever her abusive relationship and hopefully get some child support.

Clearly her self-esteem was that of a battered person under the control of an abuser. She had no car of her own, no independence, no family in the area, and no money she could access. Her husband, a long-distance truck driver, would take her to the grocery store so he could oversee her purchases. When he left on a trip, he'd leave behind the car with an empty gas tank and a twenty for her week's spending. That, though, was preferable to the irritable iron fist he wielded when he was home. He'd recently beaten the ten year old with his shoe because the boy had given him a disrespectful look. Then he took the four year old out for ice cream.

Brenda had a lot of bruises and breaks, too. She made up stories about the causes of her injuries, as well as the reasons for the older boy's broken arm. She knew the ER doctors didn't believe her, but they let her tell her tales. Her last ER visit was for a dislocated shoulder and a broken nose. Quite a fall.

She knew she needed to leave him. She even wanted to leave. She absolutely astonished me when she actually did. We had worked together to find the resources, but only she could take the action. She was terrified, but she did it. I'm sure my explanation of how Children's Services Board (CSB) would have to be involved if either boy was harmed again helped her find the strength. She didn't want to be home with her husband when CSB came knocking on the door. That would have been hard on everyone's bones.

For ten weeks, she never missed a therapy appointment. Then she disappeared. I was scared for her. She finally checked in a couple weeks later to tell me that she had called her husband so he could talk to the boys. She thought it was "only fair." So her husband came and got her and the boys and apologized, and now they were all back home together and everything was wonderful. This part of the cycle, I was to learn later, is called "the honeymoon phase."

Her Signs

Domestic violence can be one of the ways that PTSD presents itself. Typically, the abuser will be a man who has been the victim of childhood abuse, and the abused will be a woman who has been the victim of childhood abuse. These childhood traumas may have been sexual, physical, emotional, and/or psychological and may have been abusive or neglectful.

We are not talking about discipline. We are talking about abuse. When children are disciplined, they know what they did. The discipline may be extraordinarily harsh, but the children seem to understand. "I . . . (did thus or so) and the old man beat me with a board. I couldn't sit for days." This is discipline. Harsh discipline, but still discipline. This story is frequently told with a laugh. Abuse, on the other hand, comes out of left field. The abusive story usually begins with the action of the abuser: "He slammed me up against the wall because I didn't give him a morning hug!" This story is told with disbelief and disdain. Discipline is frequently tied to something a child did do. Abuse is frequently tied to something a child didn't do.

> **Discipline is frequently tied to something a child did do.**
>
> **Abuse is frequently tied to something a child didn't do.**

The domestic violence abuser will usually, but not always, be a man. The abused will usually be a woman. Men tend to act out, and women tend to internalize. Please understand that these are generalizations and stereotypes. (All we need to do is look at same sex relationships to see the exceptions.) However, generalizations and stereotypes don't make themselves up. They evolve from repeated examples.

So, Brenda, a victim of domestic violence, was *most likely* a victim of childhood sexual abuse who married another victim of childhood abuse, and he took the role of the perpetrator and she took the role of the victim. Logically, you can't have a perpetrator without a victim or a victim without a perpetrator.

And then there is the third role: that of the witness. Sometimes the witnesses are innocent, as in the case of Brenda's children. Sometimes the witnesses are complicit, as in the case of an adult family member. More likely than not, this family member/witness is the wife of the perpetrator or the mother of the perpetrator. Imagine the mother of the perpetrator, the perpetrator being perhaps the older brother, being also the mother of the victim, who, let's say, was the younger daughter. This is a scenario which is not infrequent. An all-too-common reaction for a complicit wife, mother, sibling, etc., is silence. And innocence. And lack of knowledge. This is actually understandable because some things are too horrible to know or accept. But it is intolerable and immoral. We cannot not know what we know, no matter how much we want to.

> **WE CANNOT not know what we know, no matter how much we want to.**
>
> **We know what we know -- whether we want to or not.**

All of this said, we must then conclude that in the cases of PTSD rooted in childhood abuse and neglect, we are dealing with a cycle. This cycle is often intergenerational and inordinately difficult to break. I have said to a number of courageous souls over the years, "Congratulations! You have done what no one in your family had the strength or insight to do before. You have broken the cycle!"

(You can read about the cycle of abuse by simply looking up that term.)

The previous five paragraphs were a necessary introduction--the Cliff Notes on how systems or families pass on dysfunction and how PTSD is an all too frequent result. Now, on to Brenda's signs.

Brenda came loaded with indicators of PTSD. Most telling was the symptom I have come to believe is the cornerstone of PTSD: shooting oneself in the foot. Many survivors seem absolutely unable to tolerate prosperity. When things start going well and the stars start aligning for good fortune or serenity, victims often have a great idea. For Brenda the great idea was to be "fair" to her abuser and give him a chance to talk to the kids.

I often think if victims were wrestling a snake and had the snake immobilized, they'd start feeling badly that the poor snake hadn't had a chance to bite or strangle. Their hands would loosen out of pity and a sense of how it has always been - - how we gravitate toward the familiar - - and the rattler would bite and the python would strangle. Snakes, whether reptilian or human, are notoriously lacking in the fairness gene.

Now, why victims of abuse react this way is understandable. When you have been bitten or strangled all your life, all you know is being bitten or strangled. Whatever we have predominately experienced in life becomes our normal, our reality. If we have been fed three healthy meals a day every day of our lives, then when we are left to our own devices, we will eat three healthy meals every day. If our clothes have been laundered and our living room floor vacuumed, we'll just naturally wear clean clothes and walk on clean floors. It's what we know.

If, on the other hand, we have been told we are stupid or ugly or incompetent or needy or crazy, we will act like we are all those things and attract people who will treat us as we believe ourselves to be. The abuser repeats the abuse message until, at some point, the message is internalized and the abused person becomes his or her own abuser. The message resides inside us.

We gravitate toward the familiar. It's our default setting.

So, Brenda found herself, put herself, and accepted herself in a one-down, "this is as good as it gets" position. She married what she had grown up with--control and abuse. When she worked to get herself out of the control/abuse cycle, she couldn't tolerate the dissonance, in other words, the difference between what she was accustomed to and the "new" normal, and so in her low self-esteem and passivity, she slid right back into victimhood.

Again, the reason is understandable. (At least to me, after twenty-two years of sleepless nights trying to figure it out.) Anxiety. We are going to talk more about anxiety in book two of this series, The Many Faces of Anxiety, but for now, we need to understand the following about anxiety. When things aren't normal, we get anxious. What was normal for Brenda was to be controlled and abused. When she wasn't in that familiar state, she kept waiting and wondering when it was going to come. In Al-Anon, they call this 'waiting for the other shoe to drop.' When will the alcoholic start drinking again? When will the abuser start abusing again? The only way to escape and reduce and diminish or extinguish the anxiety is to get back to normal.

Does this mean Brenda liked being controlled and abused? Hell, no. Of course not. Absolutely NOT. However, BEING abused and controlled saved her from ANTICIPATING being abused and controlled and the resultant anxiety. Will it be when he walks in the door? Before supper, when he realizes their younger son is throwing up? During supper when she has burned the rolls? After supper when there is no dessert? While watching television, when the teenager interrupts them to ask about a homework assignment? Before bed when she doesn't respond quickly enough to his sexual needs. During the night . . .

When we are waiting for something we dread to happen, the waiting, the anxiety, keeps us in a state of hyper-vigilance and hyper-arousal. We have to constantly scan our environment to see where the abuse will come from. Our radar can never be turned off. We must remain in a state of adrenalin-pulsing readiness so we can withstand the onslaught. In other words, chemically, physically, emotionally, behaviorally, intellectually, we can never relax. Until the abuse comes.

This is a gross example, but one with which almost everyone can identify. You know how good you feel right after you throw up? And then slowly the nausea and the wooziness and the aching start again and you rush back to the bathroom and sit over the toilet just waiting and watching, all tense. Your head gets hot, your cheeks flush, your back and shoulders knot, your stomach rolls, your mouth fills with saliva, your legs ache, and your heart races. You are prepared for the next onslaught of vomit. And then it comes, and mercifully you get to relax for a little bit. Your body uncoils and you break out in a cleansing sweat and you lean back feeling like a victor. You have withstood another round in the ring with Mohammed Ali.

Throwing up is in this minor way like getting abused. You can only relax when it's over. That's when you get a break. That's when you can breathe a full breath. After it's been over for a while--and how long the *while* is will be different for each victim--the tension starts building and you find yourself in an increasing state of readiness. The light slowly filters from green to yellow to orange to . . . Red. It's almost a relief when the abuse comes, because like the vomit, it allows you some peace. Until the next time.

And so, Brenda shot herself in the foot, hid in her passivity and returned to her normal, familiar state of being abused. The continual, building, unrelenting state of anxiety was too much to bear.

Her Steps

Brenda was very, very brave. She defied all the rules of control and abuse and she told. Rule #1 of being a good victim is to never, ever tell. Not anyone. Kids learn this rule really quickly when the first person they tell--often that silent, complicit conspirator--shuts them down with some version of "You're lying!" or "How can you say that about Uncle Mike?" or "What did you do to deserve that?" or "You are such a bad girl!"

Kids are also pulled into the conspiracy of silence by messages from the perpetrator: "This is our secret" or "Only grandpa is allowed to love you this way" or "You know daddy won't be able to live here anymore if anyone finds out you and I do this" or "Your mommy would never forgive you if she found out what kind of girl you are."

Brenda had held her secrets for years. It was when her fear for her children became stronger than her fear for herself that she told. And so she found a safe place: Victim's Assistance. This is one of a growing number of safe places along with emergency rooms, churches, synagogues, and, I would hope, every school in the nation, not to mention every police station, fire station and court house. "Please, help me. I'm a victim of . . ." should be all it takes.

But Brenda couldn't tell the ER docs until that one day. From there, she took, after telling, what for her was step #2: she engaged in therapy. She and I talked about what constituted abuse. Often we need someone to validate and name what it is we are enduring. "If you can name it, you can tame it," my mentor Phil used to say.

We talked about Brenda's feelings, her fears, her weaknesses, her strengths, her options. At first she seemed to simply find acceptance in therapy. Slowly she started to find some of her own inner strength. Then she seemed able to take some action to help herself and her children.

Step #3 for Brenda was to remove herself from the abusive situation. She went to the Battered Women's Shelter and began reconstructing her life. The social workers and therapists and chaplains and volunteers at such shelters have helped countless women to do this. They know what the steps are. They have group activities and group therapy sessions, both formal and informal, and many resources for support and sustenance.

Brenda was able to tolerate this for a number of weeks. And then her anxiety and her old ways of being and thinking overrode the fear for her children and the new options she had worked so hard to find.

I certainly could never blame her. I understand. Who we have been, and who we have come to believe we are, is a strong, cemented legacy. Good, bad, indifferent, it is almost impossible for us to rewrite our life script. If we do succeed in a rewrite, it is unlikely to happen in twelve weeks, perhaps not even in twelve years.

Also, it is possible that by Brenda's very act of telling, her husband will have found it wise to tone down his behavior. She broke the silence and showed him that there were things she feared more than him. It is also possible that if the abuse continued unabated,

Brenda got out again--and perhaps stayed out. She showed him a thing or two and she showed herself a thing or two as well.

My Story

The lessons here, for a budding therapist, were many. Number one is a lesson on which I have based my practice ever since: "No credit. No blame." You make changes in your life, good for you. I'm happy to walk the path with you, but I didn't accomplish the victory, nor am I responsible for the defeat. (It's great to learn humility early on in any profession!) The cycle of abuse, and, as we'll see throughout this book, the pull of addictions and the disabilities of unformed and compromised egos are greater than the skill or love of any therapist. Only a therapist, plus an open-minded, determined, courageous client, plus that magic third component (call it God, faith, hope, mercy, luck, karma, whatever . . .) can withstand and overcome the quicksand of our early imprints.

A second valuable lesson Brenda taught me is to expect and predict regression. Who among us ever learns the whole lesson in the introduction? Getting good at anything takes practice. The lessons we are trying to learn here are about appropriate assertiveness, ego strength, boundaries, the balance between self and other, trust, living in the present, and, one of the most challenging, forgiveness. Forgiveness of others, to be sure, but also, and sometimes more importantly, forgiveness of self.

A third awareness from my brief time with Brenda was the distinction between power and control. Her husband was incredibly controlling. What has become more and more clear over the years is that people who feel *powerless* latch onto people who are *controlling.*

Power is about self-control. Control has to do with forcing others to do our will. Brenda's husband controlled her by keeping her down. We empower people by lifting them up.

> *I will work on unleashing my own power so I can give up control. The person with the power doesn't need the control.*

I mentioned "appropriate assertiveness." Here's Rule #1 of Assertiveness:

DO NOT

Explain

Justify

Or

Defend.

Think about this! I am sorry to say I don't remember where I read this. If I did remember, I'd give the source credit. Let me simply say, this is a brilliant rule.

"Where were you?"

"I was at the grocery store" (Explanation)

"I had to go get milk" (Justification)

"Well, you never help me, so . . ." (Defense)

Appropriately assertive answers to the question "Where were you?"

"Why do you ask?"

"Did you need something?"

"I'm here now."

Or, "Could you put this milk away." (This is not a question.)

I remember one woman for whom I wrote down this rule in black pen. She looked at it and asked, "Then what am I going to talk about?" Believe me, if all you're doing is explaining, justifying or defending, being quiet is a great deal more powerful.

Mary

Her Story

Mary appeared in silence. She had practiced and perfected invisibility.

She was about thirty. Who could tell? Her brown hair hung over her face and eyes. Her brown glasses were all you really saw. She wore, for eleven of our twelve group sessions, a brown shirt, brown pants, brown socks and brown shoes.

The group she was part of was a research project run by the School of Nursing at a Midwest college. The counseling department had been contacted to send a graduate student to help facilitate the group. They sent me. This was my theoretical introduction to PTSD. It was baptism by fire.

The group was structured so that each week one of the participants would tell her story, and the other group members would listen, empathize, support, encourage, validate and brainstorm. I don't know how many lives the group changed. What I do know is that it changed mine.

The stories were incredibly difficult to hear. One woman told us about her father being her pimp. First, her father introduced her to drugs. Then he helped her become addicted to drugs. Then he withdrew the drugs. He would give her the drugs to which he had addicted her only in exchange for her having sex with whomever he brought home to her. He was not only her pimp, but her constant "John" as well. Her mother was elsewhere in the house when she was being raped by either her father or someone he met on the street.

Another woman told of her husband's violence and torture. She, like Brenda, said she lied to the emergency room doctors. Once, she said, she had told the truth at the hospital and her smooth-talking, maniacal husband had her committed to the psychiatric unit. The one detail of her story I remember most clearly was what she did for therapy. She cleaned her entire bathroom with Clorox and a toothbrush. It gives some indication of how dirty she felt.

A third woman's poignant story was of her and her sister and the bedroom they shared. The steps came up in the middle of the room and her sister's bed was on one side of the landing, and her bed was on the other side. She would lie still under the covers at night and listen for her father sneaking up their steps. Her mother was asleep downstairs. She would pray that just this night he would choose her sister to rape. But, then, if he did, she would writhe silently and sob soundlessly, stricken with guilt that she had prayed such a selfish prayer and that in her childlike understanding God had answered her prayer.

The story Mary had to tell was radically different. Her tormentor was her older brother. He never laid a finger on her, and he never talked to her. But from the time she was eleven until he left home eight years later to join the service, he and his friends had a little game they liked to play with her.

Her brother had drilled, hammered, knocked out, hollowed out and, in many other ways she didn't know, made holes in the floors, walls, ceilings and doors of every room in the house. Mary never knew when her brother and his friends were watching her through the peepholes.

She told her mother about it and was slapped and told never to say such things about her brother, the golden child in the family. She told her father and he said, "So? Don't do anything you don't want him to see."

For eight years, then, about three thousand days, Mary had a viewing audience. Every time she ate a bowl of cereal, read a book, watched television, scratched an itch, took a bath, changed a tampon, or looked at herself in the mirror, someone else might be watching, too. Oh, sometimes she knew for sure he was watching. Sometimes she knew for sure he wasn't watching. But most of the time there was uncertainty. Constant, predictable uncertainty.

Her Signs

It's hard to identify Mary's signs. There were so many, and they all seemed to flow into one another: hyper-vigilance; low self-esteem; inability to interact with or relate to others; lack of eye contact; soft, hesitant, mumbled speech; dullness; helplessness; lack of vitality; no trust in self or others; paranoia. You know the old joke: Just because you're paranoid doesn't mean they're not following you, or, in this case, watching you.

Perhaps Mary's most difficult symptom was her lack of interest in anyone or anything. She didn't look at anyone, wouldn't talk to anyone, never said hello or "screw you" or anything else. She simply moved through and around other people with no engagement. She held a minimum wage job as a cleaning person, which meant she was never able to emancipate and establish any independence. She was therefore doomed to live in the house with no privacy. So, she remained at the mercy of the mother who slapped and the father who blamed, and, with or without the brother, her need to stay invisible continued.

Hopelessness was her most loyal companion. She felt absolutely and eternally stuck. Her father, a deacon in a fire and brimstone church, insisted on her attendance. "If you're going to live in my home," he thundered, and then he told her the rules. So three times a week she had reinforced for her the lessons of wrath and vengeance and penitence. It also might have been mentioned once or twice that God was watching us and saw everything we did. God, also, she was reassured, was keeping a divine accounting book. All of which added up to Mary's belief: Not only was this world unpredictable and unsympathetic and unsafe--so was the next.

Her paranoia was a logical extension of her lifelong struggles. She was, reasonably, unable to trust anyone. She had no self-esteem and no belief that she herself was capable of anything other than being psychically invaded, scrutinized, observed, and, most of all, found inadequate. She felt unfit to live and unfit to die.

Her Steps

It was week ten when Mary came in wearing barrettes in her hair. It was not a flattering hair-do by any means, but we all told her how good she looked because we could finally see her pretty face. This was a huge leap of faith for her. She showed herself to the group. The turtle's head came out of the shell.

Week eleven Mary told her story. Despite her expectations, which she falteringly expressed, she was not minimized or marginalized. These other trauma survivors could not begin to imagine what eight years of day and night hyper-vigilance must have been like. We all wanted to tar and feather her parents. We uniformly found her brother despicable. And the entire group encouraged her in every way they knew how.

They talked about affordable housing, re-training programs, and existing groups which they had found and which would provide long-term support. They threw out a mountain of suggestions about self-help and self-esteem. She listened. She looked at the speakers. She cried, and she smiled.

This very vital third step, drawn hopefully from the previously unknown comradeship and compassion of the group members, allowed Mary to be able to receive. She actually absorbed our empathy, our hugs, our ideas, our presence, our honest concern for her. She took it in. She seemed that night, before our eyes and with our help, to decide she was fit to live.

Week twelve, the final week of the group, after she had revealed herself to us physically--by showing her face--and emotionally--by telling her story, Mary arrived at group wearing her hair pulled off her sweet face. Her brown glasses, her brown pants, her brown shoes and brown socks were still there, but her blouse was pink.

A note on being able to receive: As I'm writing this book, I am, of course, continuing my "day job," as they say, and seeing clients. Last night I was talking with a woman of about thirty who came rushing into my office and sat down, sighing, "Ah, peace. I can completely relax here." I asked her about her home and whether there wasn't somewhere at home that she could relax. "Only my bed," she said. Her house is almost completely bare. Nothing on the walls, nothing comfortable on which to sit. She feels she has to be prepared at every moment to leave, to run, to escape. She told me about traveling. She always wears tennis shoes and carries only one bag. If anyone approaches her or bothers her, she is prepared to drop her bag and run. (She's a professional athlete and she knows she could outrun most people.)

Now here's what I believe this has to do with her ability to receive. She cannot take inside herself any kindness, any generosity, any safety from anywhere in the world. She must always be hyper-vigilant to risk and danger. Her hyper-vigilance demands that her radar never be shut off, except when she sleeps. Because she is so busy keeping out danger and pain, she is unable to take in peace or pleasure. She is unable to receive the beauty of art work on her walls or the vibrancy of paint. She is unable to do as her husband wishes and buy comfortable furniture. She is unable to receive love. She and her husband have been married five years and have not yet consummated the marriage. In all ways, she has been unable to receive.

> *If we are busy keeping danger and pain out, we will probably not be able to let peace and pleasure in.*

My Story

The story of Mary may seem like a strange choice, but it provides us with an incredibly valuable lesson about PTSD: its variability. Not all traumas are of the same magnitude, and not all trauma survivors would be equally affected by similar traumas. What makes trauma so variable is how it is absorbed and stored in the body of the victim. I've already relayed the idea that veterans coming back from war, if they had fairly normal, loving families and fairly uneventful lives before deployment, are less likely to have as hard a time with trauma as those who were traumatized as children. This is because trauma grows on trauma. Trauma provides fertile soil for the rooting and propagation of new experiences to be stored as traumatic. Each successive trauma a person survives deepens and compounds the damage from each previous trauma.

Mary's family set her up to take the blows of life very hard. She had no support, no affirmation, no kindness, and no compassion. Her family's way of being in the world and her family's beliefs about God, that God is vengeful and punitive, denied her the existence of any softness or succor. She was born into a life of isolation and she was ill-equipped to rise above it or to separate herself from it.

The early lesson I have carried with me from this brown, broken child/woman, was very Biblical: Judge Not. We cannot know what might be stored by one human being as trauma based on genetics and environment. If we are chemically programmed for anxiety or depression, or if we have hormonal imbalances, or any of the other many vagaries of composition which make us more "fragile," we are more likely to be afflicted.

Others of us seem to have been programmed with additional resilience.

> *I am proud of my resilience. And I will not compare it to that of anyone else.*

My childhood friend, Karen, for example, who lost a teenage child and withstood incredible coldness, cruelty and lack of support from her husband for their thirty-some years of marriage, is one of the most cheerful, upbeat, positive people I have ever met.

She continues to astonish me, and she is not acting. This is who she is. What has made her so resilient, so tough, when others crumple under much lighter burdens? It's a mystery to me. But, I am aware of it and I am respectful of it. We are not all created equally in our ability to withstand the tsunamis of life. I am mindful not to judge others by Karen's standards. We'd all fail.

■

Vicky

Her Story

We are calling her Vicky. She was referred to me by someone who knew someone who knew someone. What someone forgot to mention was that I had been a therapist for only a few years. I was totally unqualified, untrained, and unprepared for Vicky.

Vicky was a lovely looking woman in her mid-thirties. She was married to a man who was oblivious to a great deal but not abusive. She had three children who loved her and had sort of normal lives and personalities. I got the picture of a family that was not tight-knit, but not uncaring. They were on the independent side and rather contently busy, each with his or her own stuff. Vicky herself was a social worker by education. By life experience, she was a woman with a multiple personality disorder. (People, by the way, who tell you there is no such thing as a multiple personality disorder, simply haven't therapeutically encountered someone carrying such a burden. In my twenty-two years, I have spent considerable time with two women who have been so afflicted.)

Vicky's dad was a doctor who sporadically took her to his office with him when no one else would be there. He raped her. Her mother, more regularly, forced her and her brother to have sexual contact with her. They were made to drink her menstrual blood in a monthly ritual. I have a graphic picture Vicky drew of this. Coming from the mother's mouth are the words, "You have to because you are so bad."

At other times of the month there were other rituals to be performed. Both Vicky and her brother were cut, tortured with ropes and chains, locked in closets and basement corners, molested and forced to memorize satanic chants and satanic worship messages. Vicky grew up in a very wealthy home in a very wealthy suburb. No one ever knew what went on behind the wrought iron gate. Her brother committed suicide when he was seventeen. It was assumed he had gotten into drugs. You know how those rich kids are.

Vicky learned to dissociate by the time she was four. Dissociating is a need-to-know talent which some people are forced to learn to save their sanity and their souls. It means, in layman's terms, leaving your body so as not to "feel" what is happening. Some victims roll over beside themselves, some cower in a corner, some float on the ceiling. It might sound handy to know. Believe me, it isn't. Those of us who don't know how to dissociate can thank our lucky stars every night that we have never been in a position where we have had to learn.

By the time Vicky was nine she had devised an army of inside friends and allies who helped her withstand the intolerable, unthinkable, unbearable, utterly despicable abuse.

Joe was the big, tough guy who came to absorb the torture.

Sarah went to school and got straight A's.

Rachel did all the eating that was done, which wasn't much because the taste of blood in your mouth and the smell of blood in your nose is a very effective appetite suppressant.

Then there was Allison who went to the office with her dad to play doctor.

Vicky's mother interacted with the very shy, very respectful Jane in day-to-day non-ritualistic times.

Vicky created a subservient, submissive "wife" who cared for the present day real-life husband.

The present day real-life children depended on a wonderfully compassionate, available woman who was the most Vicky-like of the personalities. She said she felt most comfortable as "Mom" and felt like she could be most present in that role and persona.

There were thirty-one helpers in all. Things went smoothly when they did their assigned jobs. But there was a lot of in-fighting. Joe was angry because his role of protector and tough-guy was no longer needed. Allison, who had gone to the office with dad, was known to be a slut on the lookout for some action. And some new folks had come around to drive the car, be the family accountant, and serve as the accomplished social worker.

Crazy, you say. Maybe. But what stunned me from the very first time I met her and her story started leaking out, was that this woman was walking and talking and aware of some of the lengths to which she had gone to preserve her life. She had been forced to lose her sanity to save herself. I found her to be the most creative person I had ever met. To this day, when I think of her, it is her creativity which astonishes me.

> ## *"I'm crazy so as not to be insane."*
> ### *Waylon Jennings*

I'm accustomed to the introductory phase where a client looks over a therapist and decides whether this person can be trusted. Many of the thirty-one friends came to check me out this time. In the beginning I was amazed by the different ways Vicky dressed and her different facial expressions and hairstyles and postures and ways of talking. My head was spinning. This, of course, is what she feared. I would not be the first therapist who, therapeutically, told her to go elsewhere. You've heard the expression, "Fools rush in where angels fear to tread." Well, I didn't rush in, but I didn't rush out either. I sat still. And so the helpers checked me out, some unable to tolerate anything therapeutic--too suspect--but one of the little girls bonded deeply with me and she was apparently everyone's favorite, and so, since she wanted me, I was accepted. Very provisionally, of course.

The story came out in dribbles and bits with intermittent floods of tears. The little girls desperately needed to be held. One or another would put a pillow on my lap and lay her head on the pillow and just lie still. Sometimes one would pick up my hand and indicate I was to stoke her hair. Sometimes one of the little ones would simply want to hold hands. All these behaviors would feel very natural if a small child were doing them. My intuition told me this physical reassurance was necessary, no matter how unusual and forbidden by the rules of therapeutic distance. I had never before nor have I ever since held a client's head in my lap or held hands or stroked anyone's hair. This became a therapeutic tool, though, through which Vicky and I worked on appropriate boundaries.

Violated children have had their boundaries violated, and as a result they frequently have no boundaries. By boundaries, I mean socially accepted rules of physical, emotional, conversational distance. For example, one day when I was teaching, a woman I had met once at a party came rushing up to me in the hall and said, "Will you be my friend?" Okay. Very clear. NO BOUNDARIES. Additionally, I have a client whose father-in-law put his hands down the panties of my client's five year old daughter and grasped her bottom. NO BOUNDARIES. I have another client who grew up in a house where no door was ever allowed to be closed. She had no privacy in her bedroom and no privacy in the bathroom. Nor did her brother. Their parents' bathroom and bedroom habits were all observed. NO BOUNDARIES. Books on boundaries are available. This is an incredibly complex subject with gender, social, ethnic and cultural subtexts.

With Vicky and her cast of characters we worked on trust and predictability. She hated if I was even a minute late--which would actually be early for me. She couldn't tolerate the feelings of rejection and abandonment. So, I tried to accommodate in every way I could.

For a therapist, it's like being on trial constantly. Again, I intuitively knew and understood this and remembered to feel blessed that I was the therapist here and not the survivor.

Vicky and I talked, played make-believe, read stories, wrote stories, and most of all, we did art work. It was through the art work that Vicky and I were able to track our progress.

Her Signs

We have already highlighted a number of Vicky's more pronounced symptoms. She had very tight boundaries out in public. It was impossible for Vicky to bond with friends and acquaintances. In therapy, she had weak boundaries which enabled us to talk and set goals related to boundaries in general. (This is ideally what one would hope to do in therapy: use all the information collected as a roadmap of where to go and what to work on.)

Vicky was hyper-vigilant and had a negative pattern of interpretation. She was constantly on guard, watching and discerning even the most subtle messages about herself that anyone might send. But her interpretive patterns were so negative that she constantly saw benign messages as critical and condemning. If someone frowned, she was sure she had done something unacceptable. If someone was late, as I mentioned, she was being abandoned. No matter what the information said or the number of ways it might be interpreted, she took every message personally and it all said something negative and demeaning about her.

Vicky was also co-dependent. She wanted to know all about me and my life. (This is quicksand for therapists who spend eight or ten hours a day listening to other people talk about their lives. As my mentor Phil used to say, "Therapists all suffer from ego-deprivation." So to be asked about our own lives? We have to guard against launching into lengthy soliloquies to soothe our own depleted selves.) If I had to miss a weekly appointment, she was sure I was abandoning and rejecting her, or that I would be killed in the time apart and she would not find out I had died. Finding a safe haven in her stormy life caused more anxiety for her than not having one. She was accustomed to not having anywhere to lay her head, so to speak. What she was unaccustomed to was a safe place where someone listened and cared and didn't judge or criticize. Again her pattern of negative interpretation told her she didn't deserve this, and that, for some reason or other, it wouldn't last. Every time she came, she experienced about fifteen minutes of disbelief that what I represented was still there, then about a half hour of actual relaxation and work and then the last fifteen minutes of the hour trying to talk herself through the anxiety of leaving and not trusting that I'd still be there when she came back. (Please understand that this wasn't about "me." It was about the balm a therapeutic presence offered her.)

Another symptom that must be mentioned was Vicky's fear. She was afraid of everything. Highways and back roads were equally terrifying. If she was on a top floor, the building would collapse. If she was on the bottom floor, the roof would fall in. If she was on the water, she'd drown, and if she was in the air, the plane would crash. Water was poisoned and food was covered with pesticides. All of this was absolutely understandable and rational considering what she had learned as a child. She was not safe. Anywhere. School, miraculously, was the exception. Last I knew she had two graduate degrees and was working on another.

Her Steps

Vicky was fortunately very bright and very determined. She recognized that as long as she continued with her victimization, her parents were still in control. Our goal was to regain control and empower Vicky to take control of her own life.

What can I do to cultivate a feeling of safety for myself?

>Stay in the present.
>
>Organize a cabinet.
>
>Get some exercise.
>
>Drink a glass of water.
>
>Make a to-do list.
>
>Do a lesson plan for and about safety.
>
>Create a project.
>
>Clean.
>
>Hold a teddy bear.
>
>Call a friend.
>
>Volunteer.
>
>Sit in a rocking chair and rock myself.

Our first step, as I've explained, and a difficult one in Vicky's case, was to try to gain her trust. This required a carefulness and a self-monitoring which is unusual for me in therapy or in life. I tried to move slowly in action and word, and I tried to be mindful that I was working with a very wounded child. I frequently thought of a boy I'd seen in the emergency room one night who alternately flung cursing threats and messages at anyone who came into his room and also cried for his mother. "Mommy, mommy," he would sob. I never forgot that because it became my mental poster of exactly what fear and terror can do to us.

Vicky was terror-stricken, wounded, and, I intuited, capable of anything if treated in the present in any way she might interpret as abusive. I'd already been screamed at and hit by two different clients who were dissociating. I wanted to be very careful, not for me, entirely, but for her, too. Can you imagine the guilt of having hit or hurt your therapist?

Vicky told her story. She constantly checked with me to see if I could stand it. I constantly reassured her that anything she had withstood experiencing, I could withstand hearing.

Like any good writer with too many characters, what Vicky and I needed to do was to start eliminating members of her inner circle. What had started as a supporting cast had turned into the Hatfields and McCoys. They kept messing each other up. One would keep her up all night and then she'd fall asleep in the morning and miss a final exam. Someone took the car and didn't return it for three days, during which time she was, of course, missing. She had no recollection of this block of time. (Suspend your disbelief. I can hear you thinking this is too incredible to be true. Remember, the abuse she suffered was too incredible to be true, also. And, therefore, the resulting behaviors and reactions will undoubtedly have to be as incredible as well. I think I also hear you wondering how I knew this was true. I didn't and I don't. But I couldn't dream up such a thing, could you? And whether it was factually true or not, this is what she believed happened. It was where we had to start if we wanted to get anywhere else.)

> **The only place from which we can begin any journey is where we are now.**

Vicky had the advantage of knowing what needed to be done intellectually. She had an education and training similar to mine. Knowing what she had to do was not the issue here. Transforming her intellectual knowledge to emotional strength and having a trust in others to walk through this with her was what was required. There was no necessary teaching piece here. With Vicky the challenge was to get the wisdom from her brain down into her gut. The feminists have long been quoted as saying the greatest distance in the world is from the head to the gut. It is one thing to know something. It is quite another to understand what we know so we can use the knowledge to transform our lives. Vicky and I needed to concentrate on getting what she knew out of her head and into her bone marrow. This meant she had to learn to trust herself.

I may feel like I'm in crisis. I am, in fact, simply experiencing my emotions. I have no need to fear my own emotional make-up.

We stumbled onto two major ways of proceeding, keeping her grounded and using her right brain.

Keeping Vicky grounded in the present was obviously a major challenge and one which would make all the difference to her progress. This was the beginning for me of learning to give my stuff away. I had a necklace on, a plain silver chain, the day we were talking about this and it occurred to me that I had no part in Vicky's childhood, and so anything which represented me would clearly be from the present. I took the necklace off and put it around her neck and she realized that if she wore it under her clothes, next to her skin, she'd be able to feel it and remember me, which meant remember the present.

Therapy and the therapist equal safety and the present. Any therapist and any therapy which does not equal safety and the present must be discontinued. Do not remain in any therapy situation if you do not feel safe there! If it's not safe, it's not therapeutic.

Looking at Abraham Maslow's Hierarchy of Needs will emphasize just how essential safety is.

Maslow's Hierarchy of Needs:

> Self-Actualization
>
> Esteem
> (respect for self and others)
>
> Love and Belongingness
>
> Safety
>
> Physiological needs: shelter, water, food

In reading Maslow's hierarchy of needs, we start at the bottom. We build. We as humans must first have our physiological needs met. Think of babies and their need for milk and dry diapers. Then, as we become aware that we are not the entire world, we must learn to feel safe in order to thrive. This means such things as someone needs to come when we cry. Our bed becomes our safe place. Hopefully this then translates to our home and maybe, as in my case, our village, and then perhaps gets bigger and bigger. Sometimes the safety space stays very limited. Think of the woman I was talking about earlier who said the only place she could relax was in her bed. It was, even though she was in her mid-thirties, still her only safe place.

After safety come feelings of love and belongingness and feelings of esteem. Maslow and many others say that these four basic building blocks are necessary for growth and self-actualization. Without any of the four we cannot become a whole person. We cannot flesh ourselves out and discover our uniqueness and our life purpose.

If this is a new concept for you, I encourage you to read about Maslow's hierarchy and do some self-analysis. Are your physiological needs being met? Do you feel safe? Where and with whom? With what groups or people do you feel a sense of belonging? With family? With friends? Sometimes for some people, it will only be with animals. Animals are so much better than people at showing unconditional love! Who do you respect? Who respects you? All of this is the basis from which we mature and become people of substance. It's immediately clear why therapy MUST be a safe place.

Keeping Vicky grounded required a new awareness on her part, a new paying of attention. I asked her to pay attention to the clothes she was wearing, the purse she was carrying, the watch on her wrist. These are all things that belong to an adult woman. Focusing even for a second on any one of these cues will remind her that she is no longer a vulnerable child under the control of non-protective adults. Paying attention when she was driving, when she was slicing a tomato, when she was sitting in class would help her to spend more and more time in the present. We agreed, laughingly, that when she went to the dentist she could dissociate. What a great time to leave your body and let someone else's mouth be drilled. (Just because this is deadly serious stuff doesn't mean we can't find the humor whenever possible!)

But, our real breakthrough and the most helpful thing we discovered was art work. Vicky came in one day with a picture for me. She wanted me to understand what it felt like to have this cast of characters haunting her constantly. A group of dark shapes dominated the picture. Most were black, brown and a very dark blue. Three were green and I took them to be the children. At one place on the paper was a small person with eyes--the only one with eyes. This person had no distinct shape and no distinct color, just a sort of a grey with some white and some black.

Her art work became a way for her to understand where she was. Remember Phil used to say, "If you can name it, you can tame it." Well, if you can see it, you can come to understand it, too. Psychologists use visualization especially for sports persons and actors and actresses. Picture yourself doing it, whatever "it" is. Vicky had the intuition and wisdom to do this for herself.

> ## *"If you can name it, you can tame it."*
> ### *Phil Hochwalt*

I called this using her right brain because what we want to do in therapy is bypass logic as much as possible. Very few of us have suffered wounds to our intellect. We have suffered wounds to our hearts, our emotional selves, our "inner children," as the over-used popular term calls it. Dr. Edward Tick, an expert in PTSD, says we suffer wounds to our souls. I think he is absolutely correct. His book War and the Soul is a valuable read for veterans, survivors and warriors of all kinds. It is an invaluable read for therapists, counselors, social workers and ministers of all faiths.

That picture was the first in a series of eight pictures Vicky made over a long period of time. The second picture had me in it. I was fully formed--hands, feet, eyes, smile. She remained a blob-- unformed, completely overtaken by the helpers. Gradually, as the pictures came into being, she started taking shape and the helpers began fading, becoming smaller, taking up less of her space. In the last picture both she and I were fully formed, standing with our arms over each other's shoulders.

I wish this story could end with this healing picture, but it didn't. I did something which upset her. I'd confess if I remembered what it was. She reacted in her old, familiar way. She'd been "untrusting" a lot longer than she'd been "trusting." Besides, who was I that I should be different from all the other people in her life who'd disappointed and betrayed her? The negative self-fulfilling prophesy is strong. So, she left.

My Story

Vicky left physically, but she will never leave my mind or my heart. She was one of the greatest teachers of my life. She taught me some of the most important lessons I've ever learned about therapy or life:

- Slow Down
- Be predictable and dependable. My clients are laughing, because I'm still always late! Imagine how late I'd be if I wasn't trying to be predictable and dependable.
- Suspend your disbelief.
- Appreciate every gift you've ever been given.
- Do not judge. Do not judge because we can never know.
- Keep your hopes high and your expectations low.
- Plant seeds. And know that you'll rarely get the harvest. As Mother Teresa would say: Plant them anyhow.
- Work constantly on appropriate boundaries. Without them, you will be unable to tolerate the rollercoaster of spending your days with people whose lives began and, to different extents, continue in chaos.
- Do not take your work home. Do your work, and then go home. Many of us (therapists, et al.) consider our work to be a mission, a calling, a passion, a giving. This makes it very hard to turn our professional selves off and protect our private selves. Virginia Satir, the mother of Marriage and Family Therapy, said that if we work in congruency, we will never burn out. Yes, I agree. But we also need to work in the wisdom of balance. People who toil in the human-serving professions have a hard time staying balanced because the work is never done, the project is never completed, and the semester is never over. There's no April 15th for us.
- Take nothing personally. People come and go in our lives. Be mindful that every relationship has a shelf life. Every single one. Let them come, and let them go. We meet different people for different parts of the journey and they meet us for the same. We will rarely know what they have given us and we will even more rarely know what we

have given them. Just trust in the purposefulness of the human interactions of life.

Love is the greatest therapeutic tool. Agape. Not sentimental, romantic love but the love which lives with an open heart. The love which values and respects all life. Martin Luther King, Jr., defined it this way in his 1961"Love, Law and Civil Disobedience" speech: "Agape is understanding, creative, redemptive, good will to all men." His example was that he could love the man who is bombing his home while still hating the action he is taking of bombing his home. Agape is the unconditional open-hearted love which is divine but to which we can aspire.

Vicky taught me to sit still in love and hold steady. I don't have to understand and I don't have to be in control and I am not in charge. My part is to be present in love.

■

Alan

His Story

Alan grew up poor. He was poor in every way imaginable. The second of six children born to a day laborer and a stay-at-home housewife, there was never enough of anything at his house. Not enough food, not enough beds, not enough supervision, not enough conversation, not enough attention, and not enough love. In fact, although he would never come out and say it, there was no love. There was sex, violence, chaos, manipulation, victimization, brutality, martyrdom, filth and neglect. Not much room for love.

There were two main bullies in the family and two predominant victims. Looking at a family photograph, it's easy to see who was who. The oldest brother and the father were tall, broad, scowling men. The mother and Alan were shorter, slight, and instead of anger and hatred in their eyes, their gazes were full of resignation and sorrow.

Alan's older brother practiced his boxing skills on Alan. He rarely stopped until there was a knockout. Then he'd sling Alan over his shoulder and carry him upstairs and drop him unceremoniously on the bed they shared. Alan complained to his mother one time. He was told to shut up. She had serious things to worry about.

Alan never told about the other kind of abuse. Some days when Butch the Bully was feeling magnanimous, he'd order Alan to perform oral sex on him. Or he'd sodomize Alan. Those were Alan's two options: sexual abuse or physical abuse to the point of unconsciousness. Alan preferred getting knocked out.

Other crises plagued their lives as well. Alan told about a time when he was eight and the phone rang. Alan answered it to hear a woman's voice demanding to speak to his dad. He called for his dad to come to the phone because some lady wanted to talk to him. His father left the house shortly after that and stayed away for three years. The family blamed Alan. It was three years of intense poverty. Mom took a job working three to eleven. Alan, at eight, nine and ten, made dinner for the four little ones and got them to bed. Butch was out on the streets commencing his lifelong drug habit.

Dad came back and Mom took to the couch with a meandering stream of illnesses. What cooking, cleaning and laundry got done, Alan did. For what he did accomplish, he got no credit. For what he didn't, he received constant criticism and blame.

Only three positive memories remain from his childhood. Evenings, two or three a week, or whenever he could sneak away, he'd run the six blocks to the railroad track and hop through the open door of a freight car to sleep in the peaceful, rocking, safe haven of a wooden box on wheels. In the middle of the night he'd rouse himself, roll out of the boxcar, and sit beside the track until another slow-moving train appeared going back the other way. Most people would have called it "toward home." Alan simply said, "Going back the other way."

A second positive memory was the little hideout the mother of one of his friends fixed up for him under her porch. She somehow knew something was going on and that it was awful. She showed him the opening under the porch floor. I've always envisioned one of those porches with a lattice covering between the porch and the ground. She put an old sleeping bag and a pillow there. He'd come, sporadically, to find a candy bar or a pop or perhaps a sandwich made from her family's leftover supper. She apparently never said a word about it to anyone. She simply, silently, offered him shelter. When I saw Alan as a client, this woman was in a nursing home suffering from cancer. Alan was her most regular visitor.

And the most pervasive positive memory of Alan's childhood was school. Alan was brilliant. Math, science, music, art, writing, reading--twelve years of straight A's. Alan graduated as valedictorian. He was awarded a free ride to college. Then he chose law school. He thought the greatest power for change and justice was through the legal system. All the way through school, he stood out from the crowd.

He married his high school sweetheart and opened a private practice with a few colleagues in his home town. Alan and Anne had two beautiful daughters and then a handsome, dimpled son. They bought a lovely big home with lots of land all around it. He was highly regarded as the guy you went to with any legal problem of any kind. His partners made the big bucks, but it was Alan who brought the clients in the doors.

His Signs

As an adult, everyone loved Alan. He was wise, compassionate, funny, charming and unceasingly kind. Everyone loved him. But, no one knew him. He trusted no one. Not his wife. Not his family. Certainly, not his mother. Not his colleagues at work and not his clients. Everyone was kept at a distance. He set up his life so that no one could hurt him. But, of course, they did anyhow. And, when you try to keep people from hurting you, no one can help you, either.

> **When you shut people out so they can't hurt you, no one can help you, either.**

Alan gave of his time and his expertise. He always ran late with his clients because he wanted to be sure that everyone who interacted with him got everything they needed. He needed to continue to be held in the highest esteem. No one could be dissatisfied with him or critical of him in any way. He worked tirelessly to prevent any negative view of himself. He needn't have worked so hard. He was considered the best lawyer in town, the one who could find a way to save your house or get your children out of trouble or help you sue the doctor who hadn't done his job or probate your crazy grandmother. You went to Alan with a problem, and he found a legal solution.

Somehow, though, it didn't seem to make any difference to Alan that everything he had worked for had come true. He was living the rags-to-riches American dream, but nothing was enough because nothing could fill the void his childhood of abuse and neglect had created. He was empty inside.

The first outward symptom that materialized was his eating disorder. He tried to fill that bottomless emptiness with food. The pounds slid on and then a beard materialized to hide the extra chins. He worked harder, had increasingly less time, and took increasingly casual care of himself. He was making apparent and obvious his long held belief that he didn't count. Next came a divorce, which seemed for a while to bring about some peace and a new, hard-won self-esteem. The weight came off; the teeth got whitened. An expensive new haircut and tailored clothes made him look and feel like he was taking charge of his own life. He devoted himself to his children, determined to be the best dad possible.

He was unconsciously re-parenting himself as he parented them. He played for the first time in his life.

Then came the hard-fought awareness. He was gay, not straight. He was a homosexual. What a conundrum for a lawyer, as it has always been for doctors and teachers and Boy Scout leaders and any one else we respect as a civic leader or allow to have access to our children. (This stiffly held prejudice shows such a lack of understanding about pedophilia--an ignorance, let's say. But, that is someone else's book.) Alan kept his sexual life absolutely separate from his children, his family, his friends. He worried unceasingly about being found out. His liaisons were on dark streets in other towns. His self-esteem plummeted. The cost of being gay, for him, was to live a secret life. Be true to himself about his sexual orientation? No, better to live a life of secrets and shame.

He said he was finally able to relax and feel safe when he could lie in bed with a lover after sex and rest his head on the other man's bare chest. (Remember our saying the only time a trauma survivor can relax is after the trauma? In this case, perhaps the only time Alan could relax was after a re-creation of the trauma of same gender sex.)

Alan had a client who was suing a young, attractive female attorney. He vacationed with a group of young professionals, all single, which included the attorney his client was suing. He was accused of having an inappropriate relationship with this young woman. According to the allegations, he had violated a lawyer/client relationship when he had begun a sexual relationship with the opposing counsel, which was an ethical violation since it involved a dual relationship and a potential abuse of power. First of all, Alan as an abuser of power was non-credible to anyone who knew him. Secondly, this struck me as ludicrous because those of us who knew he was gay, knew he wasn't going to be in a sexual liaison with a female.

Months later, Alan, who had been "gay" for about four years, told me that he was, in fact, dating the young woman with whom he had been accused of impropriety. His total confusion about his own sexuality, I have come to understand, is a cruel and despicable remnant of same gender sexual abuse. As if the trauma of it all wasn't horrendous enough, the resultant confusion and lack of peace about one's own sexual orientation has got to be one of the most damning legacies of this kind of PTSD.

The shame and the guilt from the allegations compounded Alan's inner turmoil and deepened his depression and heightened his anxiety. He tumbled off the pedestal of respect he had worked so hard to ascend and a vicious downward spiral of shooting himself in the foot started and seemed as unstoppable as the freight trains of his childhood. He closed the lucrative, successful private practice and downsized to a solo practice in a smaller office and then to a room in someone else's practice. He seemed unable to notice or comprehend that his clients followed him wherever he went. It was apparently too little too late. The last I knew he had taken a job in another town in a neighboring state working as legal counsel at a children's home. I've always thought it the most poignant job change and amazing metaphor. His PTSD had made Alan feel like an orphan all his life. Perhaps working with other orphaned, abandoned children would help him free himself from his childhood demons.

The big house was sold and the succession of bad business decisions and mistimed moves no doubt added to the agony of his feelings of defeat. He was still young, under forty. I can only hope that some of his later steps, those of which I have no knowledge, have proven healing and redemptive. I do know what earlier steps he had tried, and they were credible and creative.

His Steps

First of all, there were the medications. Because his brother was a drug addict, Alan was very cautious with all medications. He would try half dosages and always used as little of something as he thought might possibly help. Nothing seemed to touch his depression. To take as much medicine as might begin to make a difference, he'd start getting neurological side effects, tics, for example. His eyes would twitch as if he were having involuntary spasms of some kind.

This inability of some PTSD survivors to tolerate medication is another horrible, cruel legacy of their traumas. I believe it to be so (from my reading and workshops), because the early trauma, as we've talked about, keeps the body in a state of hyper-arousal and alters the body's chemistry and the body's sensitivity to and ability to absorb and digest all kinds of things, hence the problems with medications as well as the gastro-intestinal problems like colitis and Crohn's disease and irritable bowel syndrome as well as joint and nerve and immune system illnesses like fibromyalgia, chronic fatigue syndrome, lupus, and, probably types of cancer.

When a body is kept on hyper-alert and filled with tension over long stretches of time, how could there not be wear and tear which would break down every aspect of the working mechanism? A car which is kept running all the time in preparation for a fast get-away is going to have more mechanical failures than a car that is turned off every night and has eight to ten hours of rest before the next spin on the freeway of life.

But, try medication he did. He tried every anti-depressant that came on the market and quite a few anti-anxiety medications as well. In addition to medicine, which is the first avenue of relief, Alan tried a number of other things.

He entered into therapy with a gifted older woman in another town. He was always worried about discretion and about being "found out." He would stay in therapy for a couple months, and then he'd take a break for a couple years. He seemed as unable to tolerate the emotional/mental relief that therapy might have provided as he was to tolerate the potential relief that medication might have offered.

Alan joined a men's support group and stayed active in it for as long as I knew him. This was clearly one of the most helpful choices he ever made. While he still had trouble trusting, there were a number of men in the group who over time and with predictability came to be true friends. The men's group read books like Iron John by Robert Bly, they wrote poetry, they formed a drumming circle, and they discussed and processed their challenges as men in this time.

Alan also took music lessons and derived great comfort from being able to soothe himself with music. The discipline, the focus, the affirmation, the process, the pride in his previously undeveloped talent were all great aids to his mental well-being and all fed his spirit.

He painted his house. Again a previously undeveloped artistic talent gave him great pleasure. He chose gutsy colors and allowed himself the pleasure of experimenting with color and texture and pattern and tone. He had to sell the house, but no one could take away from him the satisfaction of having created such a joyous haven.

He threw fabulous, happy parties and surrounded himself with people who truly cared for him. As his life took its downward spiral, he closed himself off from more and more of his friends, but, again, he had proven himself capable of more than just acquaintanceship.

He also did some writing, some published, some personal, some for gifts. He gave workshops and presentations and did extensive traveling, all related to his career. These things, too, build one's reservoir of self-esteem and self-reliance. That Alan's life fell apart was not due to the fact that he didn't try with all his might to hold it together.

My Story

Alan's PTSD was horrible by anyone's standards, and his childhood had ill-equipped him for a healthy, resilient adulthood. In a family of burly, blue-collar workers, he was a geeky artist. In a hard, brittle, cynical concrete-thinking family, he was a soft, pliable, abstract thinker.

Alan, like so many other PTSD survivors, was quite adept at "faking good." He looked and acted "normal." He had appropriate social skills and could read verbal and non-verbal cues accurately. He was marvelous with his own children and with his clients of all ages and ethnicities. People considered him gifted, as, indeed, he was.

Nothing he achieved, however, was able to fill the emptiness inside. He would be quoted in the paper one day and give a presentation to his peers the next, but his successes never seemed to offer him the confidence or satisfaction to help him alter his old childhood view of himself. His childhood perceptions remained his adult reality. Nothing filled the bottomless pit of need and sorrow. He was unable to change his self-image. As the dissonance of his wise, educated, professional adulthood challenged his early poverty and abandonment, he stayed, in the mirror through which he saw himself, a powerless, loveless, deserted child.

This dissonance--what Alan had become in the present compared to how he thought of himself from the past--has become for me a measuring stick which I use to caution all other survivors. I think for Alan the disparity was far too great. The distance between where he started and what he achieved was too mind-boggling. I have imagined that if he had been a starving artist or a struggling musician as an adult, his PTSD would have been less disabling.

The great lesson he taught me, then, was the lesson in my favorite movie: <u>What About Bob</u>. Baby steps. Baby steps. Baby steps.

BABY STEPS

BABY STEPS

BABY STEPS

If we break a leg, we go from lying flat to sitting up in bed, to dangling our legs over the side of the bed, to a walker, to crutches, to a cane, to walking slowly and carefully, to walking more naturally, to walking farther, to jogging, to running on a treadmill, to running on a track, to running on a sidewalk, to . . . I'm sure I'm beating a dead horse, but you get the idea. Baby steps.

When we experience a psychic wound, we definitely need baby steps. Three of the PTSD survivors I currently see as clients I've seen for an average of fifteen years. Recovery from a psychic injury, a soul injury, is a delicate, slow process. I think Alan's great legacy to me was one of patience. And of faith. And, actually, of acceptance.

> *God grant me the serenity*
>
> *To accept the things I cannot change,*
>
> *Courage to change the things I can,*
>
> *And wisdom to know the difference.*

On a personal note, my grandmother cross-stitched The Serenity Prayer for herself, no doubt to help her try to heal from my grandfather's suicide. I think it would please her to know that this "needlework" now hangs on the wall of my home office, which doubles as my kitchen. I know it pleases me.

Roger

His Story

His father was a millionaire businessman. His mother was an executive secretary who collected shoes and fine art. No one ever molested him, whipped him or tortured him. Instead, they verbally, mentally and emotionally leveled him. They made certain he knew he was in the way. They treated him as though he were an idiot. They criticized the way he looked. They taunted him for the way he walked. They belittled him for way he "was," which evolved from no extra-curricular endeavors, no sports groups, no friends overnight. Most telling of all was his parents' disregard for the fact that Roger had no medical or dental care until he was in college and could go to the infirmary for free.

Such isolation produced disastrous social skills. Since no one ever listened to him, Roger talked too loudly when he did get a chance to talk. Since no one ever talked with him, he didn't learn how to listen. He interrupted, talked over people and, when he got an opportunity to talk, talked for much too long at any one time. He never learned how to ask questions, show approval, or validate another. Roger simply knew nothing about living in society, functioning in a group or bonding with others.

Roger dropped out of college and became a welder. But, he was unable to join a union. He didn't know how to follow rules or bend to the wishes of the majority. So what should have been a secure, financially stable life, became a constant struggle, not only financially but also in terms of being wanted and valued as an employee. And he was no one's idea of the perfect employee. He didn't take teasing, couldn't accept it or give it, had no idea how to banter with the other men, and rarely so much as nodded at another worker. He was sure, without even experimenting, that none of the guys would have liked him.

Roger, however, was flashy. He had jet-black hair and dressed only in shirts with horses on the front. His shoes were always polished and his scowl was often misread as a sexy, aloof, stare-down. That was what his wife thought when she met him. She, herself, had grown up with a critical father and, since Roger barely spoke, he seemingly wasn't going to be critical. Since he rarely interacted with people, he had no friends, and, therefore, she had no competition. She chased him, and he was thrilled. For the first time in his life, someone wanted him.

Francie was a nurse. She was accustomed to calling the shots, and to say that she was a control freak would not be overstating it. She told Roger when to work and when to stay home. When she was pregnant, he was sent to work. She found him jobs. When they had their babies, he was ordered to stay home. He later reported that the favorite times of his life were the months he spent staying home with the newborns. Newborns, as you may realize, don't care if you talk too loudly or if you talk too much. Bottles and dry diapers. He could handle it. He felt successful for the first time in his life.

Francie, however, as time went on, tired of being the designated adult in the family. When they entered counseling, one of the first stories I remember was a fight about how to make peanut butter and jelly sandwiches for the kids. According to Francie, Roger made them incorrectly. I forget what his mistake was, but I remember feeling great sympathy for him. To be criticized for making PB&J incorrectly was a new level of control in my book. She added that he did everything else wrong, too. He didn't work enough. He didn't cook enough. He didn't get the lines in the carpet straight when he vacuumed. And once he had the audacity to use a potholder to remove a pizza from the oven, and pizza sauce got on the potholder. In other words, Roger was back living with his parents. I used to get furious with him when he'd shape his thumb and forefinger into the letter "L" and put it on his forehead and repeat, "Loser, loser, loser." Of course, he had a point. That had certainly been his life experience.

As the children went through their early years and started school, Roger lost his connection with them. Mom's very negative and condemning attitude toward Dad was highly contagious. Dad began his most dependable adult coping mechanism: sleeping. He would get up when everyone went off to work or school and then go back to bed for the day. It was clear when Francie got home that nothing on the "to do" list had been touched. As she got more vocal about what a bum he was, he became more of a bum and, not surprisingly, slid into a deep depression.

The tipping point came one New Year's Eve when the kids were invited to a neighbor's house and Francie went out with some friends. When she came home, around one, Roger had taken every pill in the house and was lying across the bed, unconscious. His stomach was pumped and when he came home from the hospital, Francie and the kids went to stay with her family. The marriage was over, and Roger was on his own. More abandonment, more rejection, more neglect and more failure. It was at this point, after the suicide attempt, that Roger dragged his reluctant self into individual therapy.

His Signs

Roger was depressed. There were many days when he didn't get out of bed, didn't eat, didn't shower, didn't go anywhere, and had no break from his own negative, heavy thinking. The first thing we started working on in therapy was his own self-image and his own negative, self-defeating perceptions.

PERCEPTION IS REALITY

Perception is the individual way each of us looks at ourselves and understands reality. A loved child will look at himself as loveable and wonder what's wrong with people who don't like him. It will be their problem, because he knows he's okay. An unloved child will look at himself and know there is something fundamentally wrong with him. He expects people not to like him. He therefore meets and greets everyone with a belligerent attitude: "I know you don't like me." There's a scowl and a frown, not a smile or a nod. You don't get a chance with the Rogers of the world. They already know you don't like them, so why should they like you? They'll beat you to it. They'll dislike you first!

Now, all of this is the mind reading so common to PTSD survivors. But, here's what happens. If we mind read positively, believing ourselves to be loveable, likeable, competent and good, we'll be, most of the time, loveable, likeable, competent and good. And because we are what we believe ourselves to be, we'll face the world with authenticity, confidence and energy. And the world loves authenticity, confidence and energy. The world rewards loveable, likeable, competent and good people. There's a song from The King and I that talks about this very phenomenon. Anna and her son are about to land in Siam and everything is starting to look strange and frightening. So she sings to him--it is a musical, after all: "Make believe you're brave, and the trick will take you far. You may be as brave as you make believe you are." Psychology has a buzz phrase for this, too: Fake it 'till you make it.

Fake it 'till you make it!!!!!!

This is not about being inauthentic, believe me. This is about creating a self-fulfilling prophesy. Well, all prophesies are self-fulfilling. However, this is about creating a positive, helpful, self-fulfilling prophesy. This is not about being a cocky, glad-handing schmoozer. This is about giving the world a chance. This is about making them tell you that you can't have the job--not making them convince you that you can. This requires changing our perceptions of the universe, God, others, karma, ourselves, the cop on the corner and the lady in the post office.

Is the process difficult? You bet. As traumatized children and adults, we have learned that the world is a dangerous place, that bad things happen, and people can be mean and nasty and cruel and crazy. But, what happens to us is that we extrapolate from our experiences a perception of the whole world. We assume typically that the events of our lives accurately portray the events of all lives. To alter this assumption requires an acceptance of ourselves as posttraumatic stress survivors. The current statistic is that about 10% of the population has PTSD. We are different. We have gotten a bum deal, but it is not a constant, consistent deal the universe hands out to everyone all the time. Just because we can't see any joy in the future, doesn't mean it isn't there and doesn't exist. We'll have to work with the universe to co-create it. This is a process which begins with changing our perceptions. Because PERCEPTION IS REALITY.

> *Just because we don't see any joy in the future, doesn't mean it isn't there or that it doesn't exist. We can create it!*
>
> *We take charge of our own lives by taking charge of our perceptions.*

Now, I hear you thinking, as Roger did and does sometimes still, this is just setting myself up to be knocked down. Sometimes, yes. Everybody gets knocked down sometimes. But nobody gets knocked down all the time. One of the things that brought Roger's perceptions into clarity for me was the difference between the ways Roger describes his divorce and the way I describe mine. I say, "He left." Or I might use a nasty word in place of the 'he.' Or I might even say, "I'm divorced," admitting some accountability in the split up and not blaming the whole thing on 'He.'

Roger, however, always describes his divorce the same way: "I was RAPED," he begins, "gagged, bound and flung head first into the concrete." The casual listener would definitely not realize that this is a divorce between two consenting adults. Roger is one of those people who says, "If I didn't have bad luck, I'd have no luck."

And when his house refinancing ends up costing him more than the original offer, and when he gets rear-ended on the way to work, and when his water heater breaks, and his roof leaks, and a check bounces, and a teenager talks back, Roger is sure these things happen only to him. I don't know about everyone else, but they have certainly all happened to me.

Roger is convinced that the black cloud hangs over his head and that he alone has to experience the negatives and pitfalls of life. This attitude just helps bring more and more negativity into his awareness. Perception is reality. Once again, contrast my childhood friend, Karen, who cared for an abusive father-in-law, lived with an unemotional, unsupportive, uncommunicative husband and, most devastatingly, lost a child. Yet, she describes herself as being blessed and living a happy life.

Roger believes himself to be cursed and living an unhappy life. Roger's most difficult and persistent symptom was his ongoing obsession with suicide. He had suicidal thoughts and suicidal ideation, and he threatened suicide for most of the first fourteen years in therapy. Roger had one actual attempt and probably twenty-some threats over the years. With the threats he frequently had a plan, either pills or razors, and he always had a day and time. His plan was predicated on making someone, usually his ex-wife, and one time his children, feel a guilt and a remorse they would have to carry forever.

His passive/aggressive need for revenge is the cry of an under-empowered person against the person he or she perceives has all the power or control. The suicide, in other words, is a way to get even. Roger's plans always reminded me of the words my grandfather hurled at my grandmother on the way to the hospital where he would die three days later: "Good luck forgetting this, Martha."

Roger's impetuousness was another recalcitrant symptom. He constantly reacted before he thought about what he was doing. Someone would tease him, and he'd react with vile curses. Someone would cut him off on the road, and he'd pound on the horn and ride their bumper. One of his children would talk back to him, and he'd lose his temper.

He constantly overreacted. Those reactions came from his deep well of personal inadequacy and they were intense and extravagant. When he was attacked in even the mildest ways, his payback was poorly timed and ill-conceived. The punishment he received might have been a one on the scale, but the punishment he returned was at least a seven.

Roger was an expert at taking everything personally. If I was late, I didn't want to see him. If I was sick, it was just so I could cancel his session. If the boss at work had a suggestion or guidance of any kind, only Roger was called on the carpet. His car was singled out for parking tickets. His children were the only ones ever to tell a parent, "I hate you!"

Roger was financially irresponsible. He would shop at only the finest stores and buy only the highest quality items. Birthdays and holidays he shopped like a wild man. The children had more of everything than they could need or even want. The house was decorated to the nines and landscaped so as to be the prettiest on the block. And Roger had numerous collections. He bought old license plates and model ships for himself. This need for the unnecessary extended to his children. The girls had collectable dolls. The boys had collectable action figures.

Another of Roger's symptoms is the result of fifty years of tension and stress in his body. Physically, he is a wreck. He has high blood pressure, high cholesterol, borderline diabetes, and severe back problems which have led to hip, leg, knee and foot problems.

His Steps

Step one with Roger was to refer him to a psychiatrist. This step was met with Roger's usual personalization: "You think I'm crazy." I explained that psychiatrists are trained to understand the brain chemistry and are the best doctors to prescribe medication, and that actually, very few of the patients any psychiatrist sees are crazy. Then he tried, "You're trying to get rid of me." I explained that a therapist and a psychiatrist work together. The research is abundant that medication and talk therapy together are much more successful than one or the other. Only a psychiatrist (or a talented and willing general practitioner or internist) can intuit and prescribe medication. Only a therapist has hour-long appointments designed for listening, re-parenting, cajoling, supporting, prodding and modeling a healthy, therapeutic relationship.

However reluctant Roger was to comply, he agreed to see the psychiatrist who immediately started him on medication. I believe the first medication he tried was Effexor. It's an anti-depressant which generally has an energizing component. It immediately worked. I have observed that the more a person needs an anti-depressant, the more quickly it seems to work. Unfortunately, for Roger (Remember, if he didn't have bad luck he wouldn't have any) it had side-effects which to him were intolerable. Multiple medications were tried.

Some worked; some didn't. The psychiatrist was amazingly patient and determinedly creative. He designed anti-depressant/anti-anxiety cocktails for Roger which lost their effectiveness after about six months. Most people build up a tolerance to an anti-depressant after about ten years. Six months for Roger.

The difficulty with finding medication which worked and was tolerable for him was not surprising. We talked previously about the long-term effects of tension and stress on the body and mind of a PTSD survivor. Many medications don't work or work differently for PTSD survivors due to the way the body chemistry has been over stimulated and unable to rest and recover from episodes of hyper-alertness and overdrive. Roger's psychiatrist, for example, in an attempt to get him out of bed and moving, prescribed Ritalin. For a person who does not have attention deficit disorder, for which Ritalin was long the drug of choice, Ritalin acts like speed. It had no effect on Roger... No effect whatsoever. We were all stunned. What an unforgettable lesson in how PTSD shocks and changes the body and mind chemistry.

In therapy, work on Roger's depression began with identifying, understanding and changing perceptions. This was about as speedy as building the pyramids one stone at a time. We set about identifying and working on altering his negative self image, his negative self-talk and his negative projections on others. One of the ways we worked on this was that for about six months I wrote out and gave Roger flash cards at every session. His assignment was to read them over first thing every morning and last thing every night before bed. This assignment was predicated on my encouragement that he actually get out of bed every day. Here are some of the messages on the more than 100 cards:

Perception is reality.

What have I learned from this?

I don't have to compare myself to anyone else.

No one can treat me like crap without my cooperation.

Status quo is the way Roger wants it to go-- But not the way Roger will grow. When no one calls me back or responds to my needs--I will dig inside myself and know that an answer is available if I just listen.

I hold a high moral standard and am ethically accountable for my behavior.

The wisdom is inside my head and heart.

I'll feel whatever I feel without judgment.

The children will teach me all I need to know about joy.

I'm a good person.

I deserve happiness.

These flash cards differ from affirmations. Affirmations are written according to various guidelines which work with the mind on positive messages. Affirmations are a helpful way to pull ourselves out of the doldrums and spiff up our self images. They, I thought, were too divergent for Roger--too far from his reality. We had to start closer to home. Typical affirmations include wording such as: "I am a beautiful person." "I enjoy life." "I find the best in every situation." Roger wasn't quite ready to start there. So we specially designed cards which were palatable for him.

A great deal of therapy with Roger would have seemed to a casual observer like superficial chit-chat, and in many ways it was. Roger had no template for normalcy. He didn't know what a normal parent/child relationship was like. He had never had a friend, and was awkward in attempts made both by others and himself. He had boundaries which varied from the overly rigid, allowing no one near, to the overly loose, which amounted to scaring people away because he seemed so needy. Therefore, a lot of what we talked about over the years dealt with the definition of normal. I have often wished there was a book about normal. Perhaps that could be my next writing project. People who grow up in abuse, neglect, criticism, condemnation, total permissiveness or total denial, grow up with no idea of the wide and flexible middle ground that makes up "the normal."   For example, never giving a child any idea of what he or she is doing well is not normal. But where are the limits? Never reprimanding or guiding a child is equally harmful. One of the things Roger and I talked about is the distinction between approving of the child as a person and approving of the child's behavior. The child has to be valued for himself or herself but also has to know that not everything he does is acceptable. I remember friends telling about the man who had season tickets to the symphony in seats directly in front of them. He apparently made distracting noises and produced toxic odors during every concert. He may have been a perfectly acceptable human being, but his behavior made my friends grow to dislike symphony music.

Remember the Robert Fulghum book, <u>All I Really Need to Know I Learned in Kindergarten?</u> That may be one of the only books ever written which talks about normalcy: Share. Rest. Take turns. Hold hands and stick together. What wonderful nuggets of basic human behavior. They seem, well, obvious, but Roger was missing a lot of the basics which most of us learn by osmosis from our parents and families. As I said earlier, Roger talked too long at any one time. Such behavior isn't normal. And the world is very hard on people who don't act normal. You can be as screwy as a fruitcake in this world of ours, as long as you know how to act within the normal range.

Roger filled many a journal in those early years. First he spilled out story after story of long-ago hurts and heartaches mixed in with present-day pain. Then he started using his journal to capture his feelings and behaviors so we could talk about them. Was this oversensitive? Was that overly harsh? Had he, indeed, been mistreated here? Was he out of line there?

Along with such self-analysis, Roger took another step to help in his PTSD recovery. He filed bankruptcy and gave himself a fresh start financially. He came to understand that he was an emotional spender as well as an emotional eater. He works to keep both under control.

My Story

Probably the least therapeutic reaction I ever had in my life was to Roger's suicide threats. He would say, "I'm going to off myself." I would say, "You can't." I used unabashed guilt to try to keep him from killing himself. "You chose to have children," I reasoned. "Once a person makes that choice, they invalidate the choice for suicide." I told him about my grandfather killing himself and about the consequences through the generations that the one act of desperation caused. Again, he would say, "I'm going to." Again, I would say, "No, you're not. You are not leaving your children with that legacy." Round and round we would go.

What finally stopped that merry-go-round of Roger's stubborn desperation and my equally stubborn desperation was a deal we cut. He was determined to commit suicide on the day after Thanksgiving. I managed to get him an appointment with an internist on the Saturday after Thanksgiving, and he agreed to wait twenty-four hours before proceeding. This amazing doctor spent two hours with him on that Saturday afternoon and I have not heard the "s" word since. This physician looked at him with fresh eyes and started treating the physical and the mental issues Roger presented. That physician has been tireless ever since. It's almost two years, and the difference in Roger is incredible. He has hope. For the first time, he has hope.

Roger and I have had a turbulent decade and a half as client and therapist. He has taught me more about patience and temperance than any other client. He comes in on rants and it's all I can do to keep my mouth shut. He rails against those who have hurt him and his narcissism drives me to distraction. He is convinced he is the one person in the world who has received the worst treatment the world has to offer. He has threatened to leave and never come back if I mention the starving Armenians again. He has also threatened to make sure my license is taken away, to call me at home in the middle of the night, to . . . You name it. Then, another day, he tells me he's a "lifer" and he'll be my last appointment on the last day I practice. It has been a wild ride. But, after all these years, I think we have come to trust each other. I sometimes think it is even more amazing that I trust him than that he trusts me. Perhaps both are remarkable and perhaps they could only happen in tandem one with the other.

A last symptom of Roger's which was too personal to me to put in the symptom section and had to be reserved for my story was Roger's expressed hatred of God. Roger grew up with no religious training at all but in college found a church he loved. When he met Francie, they were both devout, practicing Catholics. They were married in the Catholic Church and attended mass regularly. Roger considered himself a faithful follower.

With the divorce and the resultant devastation of his adult life, Roger decided God was a punitive, miserly God who withheld and taunted and turned his back on the likes of Roger. Probably the one issue Roger and I talked about more than any other was God. Free will was a new concept to Roger, an age-old one to a catholic like me. The catholics who go by the lower case 'c,' I remember learning in catechism, were those believers of the ancient, undivided, universal Christian church. So his Catholic and my catholic have had an ongoing dialogue about God.

The last time I saw Roger he was telling me about one of his children who has been debating whether or not he wished to be confirmed in the Catholic Church. Roger's teenager was really disgusted that God let bad things happen and he wasn't sure he wanted any part of it. Roger listened to the concerns with respect and patience. Then he started a dialogue with his child on free will. After a few days of thought the decision was made to go ahead with the confirmation. Roger is glad. He handled a difficult situation with tact and diplomacy. Whew. I have to enjoy this baby step while I can. I'm sure Roger and I will be back on the roller coaster the next time I see him. I feel like I'm the "lifer."

Olivia

Her Story

Olivia arrived on an emergency basis, the friend of a friend of one of the psychologists in the office. The friend had called to ask if someone could see Olivia ASAP. I'll never forget the first thing she said to me: "I think I'm crazy." I had never seen anyone in a full-fledged anxiety attack before. It was not a pretty sight. Her body was shaking violently. I tried to hold her hands but they were moving so much they wouldn't stay in mine. I put a hand on her leg and could feel her legs twitching uncontrollably. I simply scooted my chair up next to hers so we were knee to knee, and I held on to her as much as I could while she shook and tried to talk and cried and hiccoughed and coughed and sweated.

I assured her that she was having an anxiety attack and that she wasn't crazy. I explained: "The folks who know these things always say that crazy people don't know they're crazy. So if you think you might be crazy, you're not, because if you were, you wouldn't realize it." Whether that argument had any effect, I don't know, but the shaking gradually subsided and the shudders spaced themselves farther and farther apart. One of the ironies of that first visit was that her father brought her. I was to learn, as the story unfolded, that it was her father who had abused Olivia, her older siblings and her mother. Of course, on that first day we didn't talk about what had caused this onslaught of anxiety. We talked simply about coping skills for recognizing and reducing it.

Olivia is a bundle of unrealized potential. She is a beautiful woman with luxurious hair and flawless skin who has no idea she's beautiful. She is model slender and walks like the dancer she always wanted to be. She is bright and resourceful and resilient but has had little opportunity to realize any of those possibilities. Born into another family, Olivia would probably have become a teacher in one of the arts or humanities. She is tied with my father as the most honest person I have ever met in my life. She is compassionate, intuitive and gradually coming to learn and accept that she is psychic. (We'll come back to Olivia's psychic ability later.) In her family there was zero support for realizing potential and seeking opportunities.

One of her childhood stories is about being sent around the neighborhood with an old doll carriage to collect food for the poor. She then brought the food home and her mom used it to feed her own children who were, indeed, impoverished. Olivia remembers breaking up the furniture to burn in the fireplace during the winter. She, like so many other abused and neglected children, had no dental care and only life-and-death medical care. The first time she went to the dentist she walked, carrying money she had earned herself in her after-school job at the drugstore.

This will sound familiar from Alan's story, but the physical poverty which was present when her father was absent was much preferable to the physical abuse which filled their lives and minds when he was present. Dad had been the scrawniest of seven boys in his family and he, himself, grew up witnessing a lot of physical violence and being the recipient of an enormous amount of pent-up anger and hatred from his own father. He learned of cruelty from his father to his mother and witnessed cruelty from his father to each of his brothers who, in turn, came after the next youngest in the age-old enactment of the shit rolling down the hill. It piled up on the boy who became Olivia's father..

The cruelty in this family seems to have been generations old, as information about her grandparents can attest. Olivia's grandparents probably would have had more than seven children but fate intervened. Grandma liked being pregnant. It was the only time that grandpa kept his hands off her, physically and sexually. Of course, he had a practical reason as well. Grandpa was hell-bent on having enough workers for the farm. It's not surprising that a man who sees his children as free labor should hate to spend money. After grandma had three children with the help of the community doctor, grandpa decided the doctor was a waste. He, himself, would deliver the babies. Four, five and six were no problem. Number seven, Olivia's dad, was premature. Even when it was abundantly clear that things weren't going well, grandpa brought the baby into the world, took the cradle near the fireplace to warm up the little guy, patted grandma on the arm, told her to rest and left the room. Olivia's uncles told Olivia's father that they had heard their mother screaming, and then whimpering, and finally, moaning. Eventually everything was still. Their father forbade them from entering the room. In the morning, when grandpa went back into the bedroom with the squalling baby, grandma lay still and stiff. He called the boys in to say goodbye to their mother and then sent them out to dig a grave.

Grandpa reportedly tried diligently to find a replacement mom for this mob, but no one was willing to take on seven stepsons, including a scrawny, undernourished baby, much less take on grandpa, whose reputation had preceded him all over town. Olivia learned all this from a father who bragged about it, almost revering his father when he was sober, and cried about it with fathomless self-pity when he was drunk.

From this beginning, Olivia's dad came into adulthood a belligerent, angry, raging man. A stint in the Army didn't soften him any. He became a long-distance truck driver whose company demanded that he unload the trucks himself. This added a violent twist to his behavior as he frequently treated the children with as much brutality as he treated the boxes he was unloading from his trucks. Olivia, like him the littlest and lightest, went farther across the room and was hurt the most when he hurled and heaved the children around.

Her two older siblings left home as soon as they possibly could. Neither graduated from high school. Her older sister got pregnant and then got married and then got out of the house. Her older brother falsified papers somehow and got himself into the Navy. He became a submarine mechanic. In a rare moment of vulnerability with Olivia, he explained to her that he felt safe on a submarine. Their absconding left Olivia, at the age of nine, alone with an un-empowered mother and a cruel, controlling, abusive father.

Olivia calls her troubling childhood memories "Kodak moments." She has flashes that don't make much sense to her, but she sees each flash in her mind with the clarity of a photograph. She is crawling silently beside the sofa where her father is sleeping and his hand juts out and slaps her in the head. She is riding in the backseat of a car which her father is driving fast and erratically, knocking over trash cans and sideswiping mailboxes, when a woman's gloved hand comes over the front seat and pushes Olivia down on the floor in the back and holds her there. Now, as an adult, she knows it was her mother's hand trying to protect her from what she must have felt was an imminent accident. She has a clouded image of an oriental woman smiling at her as her father introduces them. She remembers getting into the car ostensibly to go get ice cream and ending up at the hospital to get her tonsils out instead. She has a memory of a doctor with bushy eyebrows and a mask and wonders if this is connected to the tonsillectomy.

She has another ice cream memory. They are driving to get ice cream, she and her parents and the two older ones, and her mom says something to her dad, she can't hear what, and her dad slams on the brakes and turns around and without explanation drops everyone off at home and keeps going himself. These Kodak moments come without warning, flash in front of her mind, and drive her to distraction. "What is all this stuff?" she wants to know. "What does it mean? Why won't it stop? What can I do? See, I'm crazy."

Olivia has an album of memories which haunt her days and shatter her sleep. One of the most upsetting happened when, she believes, she was eleven. Her father and mother had one of their many unbalanced fights. Her dad was more angry than usual and beat her mother with his fists. Olivia was in the house while this was happening, but her parents were in the bathroom and the door was locked. Her father finally flung open the door and flew down the steps and out of the house. She found her mother unconscious in the bathroom. She remembers dragging her into the bedroom and somehow getting her into bed. Had her mother not been moaning, she would have believed her to be dead. Olivia cleaned her up and nursed her as well as any eleven year old could, and then she spent the night sitting behind the front door with a large butcher knife in her hands. He was not going to hurt her mother again.

The fighting was so bad that whenever possible her older sister would come and get her and take her to her house for the weekend. Olivia had a room to herself at her sister's house. She would frequently wake up to find her brother-in-law standing silently in the room, and when she would say something, he would say he was just checking on her and walk away. Then one night she awakened to his hands rubbing her legs and removing her panties. She screamed and ran the mile home in her pajamas and bare feet in the middle of the night. Despite the fact that she told her story with outrage, the family version of that night was that Olivia had had a bad dream and, in her usual, super sensitive, overly reactive way, made a mountain out of a molehill. Nothing had taken place.

This happens all too frequently to PTSD child victims. They are not believed. Insult is added to injury.

Finally her parents divorced and Olivia and her mother lived on scant child support but the joy of no violence and no fear. The abuse had taken a toll on her mother, though, and her incredibly mistreated and abused body was no match for the cancer that came. Olivia nursed her for the three years that it took the cancer to kill her. By this time Olivia was just graduating from high school and so, with her options an abusive father's house, her sister's house where her brother-in-law was free to molest her, or a stowaway on the submarines with her brother, Olivia chose her life path. Having completed a medical technology class in the vocational high school she attended, she took the first full-time job that was offered, in an obstetrician's office, and found herself the cheapest apartment in town. She was never to escape the cycle of poverty known as the working poor.

Olivia married once. Her husband was so respectful that he told her he wanted to wait until after they were married to have sex. He was a musician and he was temporarily between gigs. He didn't have a violent bone in his body. She dragged him with her to meet me. Neither of us imagined that he was gay. Three years later, with an unconsummated marriage and a couple thousand dollars of extra debt, she asked him to leave and the marriage was over. It had been a non-violent relationship and an affectionate one. Had Olivia not been so impeccably honest, she might have been able to tolerate the fraudulent nature of the non-marriage.

Single ever since, Olivia has gone through periods of great emotional contentment and periods of horrendous upheaval and loneliness. As her symptoms materialized, we tried to handle them.

Her Signs

Anxiety was and has always been Olivia's primary and most disruptive symptom. It was anxiety, in fact, which proved to be the tipping point which brought Olivia into counseling. It is just so very hard for her to ever feel safe or relaxed. Her early childhood of pain has so tightened and constricted her body and her mind that she is a chronic jangle of nerves and tension. If she has something to worry about, she obsesses about it. If she has nothing to worry about, she worries that she's missed something and she becomes more hyper-vigilant and wired.

She describes in her own written words what happens to her and how unexpectedly it happens:

> I went to have breakfast with a friend. We sat and ate and talked about nothing in particular. I said, "I must have had too much coffee. I feel jittery." When we were standing in the parking lot saying good-bye, I could feel a "rush" through my entire body. My throat became very tight, felt swollen, my hands were shaking, my legs shaky. When I got in the car, I felt weak, sweaty, and nervous.
>
> Driving home I began to feel fearful, then scared to the point of crying. I stopped to get cigarettes. As I reached for the door of the store, there was another "rush." I couldn't help thinking, "Why are you afraid of a door?" Then it occurred to me to try something. When I stood in line, I stayed still, touched nothing. Bam. Another "rush."
>
> Panic, fear, shaking. However, I realized that my "rushes" occurred on their own. Doors do not trigger them.
>
> Lines of people do not trigger them. I came home, went to the bathroom, felt faint, then laid across my bed. My thinking was confused, fragmented.
>
> Bits and pieces of conversation popping in and out of my head. One-liners, so to speak. I sat up, afraid. The room looked slightly distorted. Judgment of distances slightly off.
>
> I looked at the clock and was aware that my perception of time was off. I thought maybe it had been an hour. It was ten minutes. Then the feeling of drunkenness mixed with nervousness. I could feel myself becoming "drunker."
>
> I slept for two hours. Awoke feeling shaky, hung over, jittery. It lasted another hour or so. Then I felt fine again.
>
> It's much later now and it's over. I'm not terrified and I don't feel crazy. So how about a little humor. Maybe this is some kind of Scarlett O'Hara Syndrome. S.O.S. Didn't all those southern belles occasionally come down with a case of the "vapors"?

Clearly you can tell from Olivia's writing that her sense of humor was not one of the things she lost to PTSD. Her descriptions of being drunk on anxiety were eloquent and very helpful to her when she was able to make the perceptual leap from victim to observer. Stepping back to describe herself in a journal is one of the steps we took to work with Olivia's symptoms. It makes more sense to talk about it here than to come back to it in the next section. This switch from being inside something--a participant or a victim--to being outside something--an observer or a survivor--can strengthen resiliency and move us from our emotional state to a thinking one.

Take a half step back

And become an observer

Instead of a participant.

Neurological research explains what actually happens inside the brain. Put simply, whatever parts and paths of the brain we use most are the ones that develop most completely. When a child is traumatized, the part of the brain that develops is the part which allows for an immediate response without thought or hesitation. This creates what is often seen as a hair-trigger reaction to insult or injury. There is no time for thought, and so, in fact, the brain doesn't engage any thinking parts. It responds. The response is often not appropriate, but, then again, there are few appropriate responses to being beaten, battered or raped. So traumatized children learn to act and react without thinking about their actions or reactions because, bluntly, abusers don't tend to negotiate.

In a dead heat with her anxiety as the hardest symptom she's had to deal with comes Olivia's depression. Again, her descriptions are poignant.

> I hoped today I would wake up with a better feeling. I didn't. I try to keep busy with cleaning and reading. But, I can't seem to shake the feeling. I'm 36. I know that's not old, but things haven't turned out how I expected. Fifteen years ago

> I would have thought I'd be somewhere else. I thought financially things would be better. I thought maybe I'd be

married and have   a couple of kids, like everybody I know.

There's just always this feeling of foreboding. Afraid of what's to come. I don't know any other way to explain it.

I want to be happy. I want to be optimistic, enjoy things. I just can't seem to shake these feelings.

I don't understand myself anymore. That frightens me. I try to act like I used to act, thinking that if I "act it" I will become it. But deep down inside it's all changed. I'm afraid. Somewhere I'm afraid I'm going to die soon. I know this doesn't make sense. I'm fairly young. Up until recently my health has been pretty good. I'm just afraid I don't have much time left. Isn't this crazy? It doesn't make sense to me. I don't want to die. I don't know what's wrong with me.

I never used to think crazy thoughts like this. Maybe I did go crazy.

Maybe I just did it so quietly, no one noticed.

Many things in Olivia's writing leap out at me as I read it over eighteen years later. Her sense of loss and grief, her regrets, her feelings of being different from others; her feelings of craziness because she has reactions and responses which make no sense in the non-traumatized present; her confusion about what PTSD is and how it affects so many aspects of her life; her pervasive fears; the constant looming of things dark and inexplicable and undeserved--even to the point of death; and her belief that she is invisible. No one would even notice if she died.

Her mental state of constant alarm has wreaked havoc with her body as well as her mind, altering her body chemistry. As expected, she has physical problems which also plague her day in and day out. It seems she no sooner gets one problem under control than another arises to keep her from feeling healthy physically. She has had serious thyroid problems. She has had constant gastro-intestinal problems. Her first memory of gastro-intestinal issues was when she was very young and she was crying because her stomach hurt. She remembers her mother rocking her and trying to soothe her, whispering, "It's only hunger. It'll go away soon."

She has had a constant slew of gynecological problems, as well, which resulted in her meeting an incredibly important man in her life, her primary care physician, a compassionate man with strong, appropriate boundaries and an interesting twist on almost everything. This is another example to me of the way in which PTSD survivors often encounter people who are amazingly good and constant. It's as though the universe wants to make up to them for the early awfulness of human mistreatment.

Another symptom I want to point out is her dissociation. This is very evident in her Kodak moments. Remember she sees herself crawling, sees herself being pushed down in the back seat of the car, just as she sees herself in the other flashes. In her flashes, she is outside her body, viewing herself in the picture. When these things happened in real time, Olivia dissociated. She left her body. This is a characteristic you'll remember from Vicky's story. Wikipedia provides a clear explanation: "Dissociation can be a response to trauma, and perhaps allows the mind to distance itself from experiences that are too much for the psyche to process at that time." In a massive understatement, the blurb concludes that dissociative episodes "tend to be quite unsettling."

Her Steps

Many of Olivia's steps have been helpful, creative and resourceful. But, in my opinion, they have all been conducted with her hands tied behind her back. From the first day I saw her until last week, Olivia has vehemently and totally refused medication. We have gone round and round about this, and finally she wore me down and I stopped arguing with her. Having seen enough of the vagaries of medication's effectiveness for PTSD folks, the ways it reacts with stressed-out chemistry, the way it produces a quick tolerance, I have to reluctantly admit that she may have been very wise to proceed without medication. She was adamant. With her "rushes" and her "flashes" and her "drunkenness," she was unwilling to fog up her mind in any other ways. I don't believe that's what anti-depressants and anti-anxiety medications do, but, perhaps for her, that is exactly what would have happened. So, contrary to the well-researched "talk therapy plus medication gets the best results," we plowed ahead on our own.

Olivia has been absolutely constant in therapy. In the more than eighteen years, I have probably seen her forty-eight weeks a year. She has tried every suggestion, with the notable exception of medicine, and has read volumes of recommended books, written journal upon journal of memories and thoughts and doubts, exercised, drawn, taken yoga classes, challenged herself to go away overnight with girlfriends, gone to classes and groups and workshops. She, like so many others, has tried many different things to help herself heal.

Olivia said recently that she thinks the single thing which has helped her the most in her recovery was the contrast of my way of working with her and that of her general practitioner She would say to me, "Do you think I'm crazy?" and I would reply definitely, "Absolutely not." She'd say to him, "Do you think I'm crazy?" and he'd reply quizzically, "So what if you are?" I'd send her to the library to find a book on creative journaling, and he'd send her out to the woods to collect bird feathers for him. I'd suggest she get a part time job in a flower shop, and he'd suggest she plant a garden. Now, if it were me and I had two health care professionals giving me such divergent advice, I think I'd have ditched one of them. Not Olivia. Somehow she finds it helpful and healing. Even funny, maybe. Crazy "experts." Maybe that's it. Maybe he and I are helping her to feel less crazy because we're both sort of wacky.

My Story

I remember the day, about three years ago, when Olivia stormed into my office for her appointment and snarled at me, "I am so mad at you!" The why turned out to be that I had finally convinced her that she wasn't crazy. A family that doesn't believe a child, especially one who would run away in the middle of the night in her pajamas, is a crazy family. Olivia fumed, "It was much easier when I thought it was me. Then I could do something about it. What do I do about this?" I suggested Wyoming. She obligingly laughed.

Olivia has since retired from her first and only full-time job and has found some interesting and safe part-time jobs. She still struggles with finances, but she has never paid a bill late and is generous with those in worse shape than she. I remember the time she went to the warehouse store because she had heard on the radio they were selling blankets for $2 apiece. She bought ten and gave them to a shelter.

She has a few very good friends, including her two health providers, has set increasingly self-loyal boundaries with her family and friends, and continues to read voraciously, watch intelligent television, feed the animals in the woods behind her apartment, and content herself with her peaceful existence. She has some anxiety still, but she views it differently, and she has some depression, but that, too, she takes less seriously, knowing it so intimately that she now trusts both will go just as they come, here and there, but not always.

I recently came across a mental health test Olivia took in 1992. The results suggested that she might refuse to cooperate in therapy, was extremely defensive when talking about psychological material, would adapt poorly to environmental changes, was submissive, yielding and powerless, was likely to be with men who were sadistic and abusive, would most likely be a victim and a martyr, and was in gross denial and repression. I am thrilled to say that seventeen years later, not a thing that test projected is true. And all of this without medication.

I often tease with clients when they have an epiphany or make some great stride that I wish I had a bumper sticker announcing, "Most improved client of the month." If I did, I'd give it to them. Olivia would be in the running for "Client who has worked the hardest and come the farthest." What amazing courage she has demonstrated.

P.S. I mentioned her psychic abilities. I want to expand on that fleeting remark.

Those who find themselves in a traumatic situation once tend to be obsessively on the lookout for the danger signs that might indicate the trauma is about to happen again. This obsessive looking is a coping mechanism, a preventive form of paranoia. It is about to happen? There was no moon that night. Can I see the moon? It was raining. Is it raining? I could smell gasoline. Can I smell gasoline now? There were furtive sounds that made me think of a stalking tiger. What can I hear? Now, to complicate things a little more, this whole process of hyper-vigilance which scans the environment and surveys for danger is done unconsciously and fast, fast, fast. Those who have been repeatedly traumatized, or perhaps traumatized in different ways, learn to scan for everything. They constantly scan the radar. Trauma victims become very good at this. They often become so good at this that it becomes second nature. It becomes a constant habit. It becomes a way of life.

To have had to learn to be so compulsively observant, so obsessively watchful, is to be able to anticipate who people are and what they might do before they ever begin anything. Trauma survivors can smell danger; they can feel repressed anger in the hairs on the back of their necks. They can read people. Their lives have depended on it.

I remember the woman who taught me this. When I worked at Victim Assistance my job was to run a supervised visitation program which was court ordered when there were allegations that a child was unsafe with a parent or grandparent. Students from the social work and counseling programs at a near-by university did the actual supervision of the visits. I interviewed the parents or custodians of the child or children. I had to gather data and fears from the one parent and then interview the parent who would be supervised to explain the rules and to try to assess the level of danger the supervised parent might present for the child or children and the supervisor.

One of the student supervisors stood out from the rest. Her reports were more detailed, she observed more pertinent information, and she picked up small gestures or vocal cues the rest of the staff, me included, were likely to miss. I started asking her to come to the "accused" parent interviews. She was astonishing. She could tell from passing a person in the hall whether they were dangerous or benign. We had this one innocent-looking grandmother come in, wanting visits with her grandchildren. Barb, the student supervisor, leaned back in mock horror when the white haired seventy-year-old left my office. "She is so inappropriate with those children," Barb told me later. "Are you psychic?" I asked her. "I guess so," she shrugged. "PTSD survivors have to fine-tune every ability to read between the lines. I guess some of us cross over after we've practiced enough."

Ted

His Story

Ted was an incredibly popular college professor. Every couple years he was voted the best teacher at the school. His classes were always filled. He was bright, acerbic, colorful, playful, demanding and energetic. He was a runner. He was happily married with children. Life was good, at least as far as an outsider could tell. The reality was somewhat different.

When Ted came home from his classes, he went to his study in the attic. He didn't greet his wife, didn't interact with his children, didn't eat supper with them, didn't read to them or tuck them in or help them out. He just roomed there. Once in a while he'd watch some television or a movie with them. Mostly, he meticulously graded student assignments and prepared for the next classes, also meticulously. When everyone was in bed, he'd go down to the kitchen and fix a sandwich or some soup and eat a solitary meal. Then he'd stretch out on the living room floor and sleep. He slept with his eyes open, his senses heightened, his weapon, whatever it was that night, within reach.

He'd awaken before anyone else, shower, grab his books and head off to the university. He'd be in his office by six, feet on his desk, reading. He loved to learn. His mind was jammed with stories and theories and facts and statistics. Later, as the other professors straggled in, Ted had the coffee waiting.

Weekends were different. The lawn would be manicured, the gutters would be cleared, not a fragment of debris remaining, and the pool would be cleaned and ready for the kids. In the winter the snow would be shoveled and the firewood split and stacked and the furnace filter changed precisely on the night of the last day of the month.

These activities were the extent of his family involvement. For example, if his wife and kids had things to do over the weekend, he wouldn't go along. He was too busy with school work. He was working on a third advanced degree and then he had his teaching. Occasionally, if the kids needed to be taken to games or events or hikes or camp outs, he'd be glad to take them. However, he then stayed in the car and waited for them. In his mind his actions proved that he loved his wife and kids. He did everything in his power to protect them and provide for them.

His wife was lonely to the core. She was a single mom with a strange man in the attic and a great handyman who required no instruction. She had had cancer as a young woman and had an artificial leg. She blamed his distance on her disability. Nothing could have been further from the truth. But, her disability and the low self-esteem that resulted from his polite, superficial treatment of her kept her a captive in her own home. She babied and coddled the children and made them her life. She knew who was where at all times and who had what to do for homework and which socks they each had worn that day. When everyone left home for the day, she sat and smoked and drank coffee. She was horribly depressed. But it was her secret.

Ted had a secret, too. He was addicted to marijuana. When he got up before dawn, he smoked a joint. When he finished his run in the afternoon, he smoked a joint. When he came home and headed off to the attic, he smoked a joint, and when he stretched out on the floor to try to sleep, only another joint could relax him enough so he could even lie still. Ted was a Viet Nam vet. He had been a commanding officer for eighteen months, until the last round of wounds sent him home for surgeries and a Bronze Star. He had continual flashbacks, haunting nightmares, and found himself unable to bond with, trust, talk to, listen to, hug, hold or love anyone. He was a shell of a man. Functioning, to be sure. But how he kept going was a mystery.

When his wife could stand it no more, she demanded that he have therapy, and not at the Veteran's Administration which had been the only therapy he'd tried before.

In he came. I was about to experience what a wonderful teacher he was, although it was not his intention to teach me anything. To say that he didn't want help would not be true. He understood quite accurately that there were few civilian counselors who would have any idea how to help him. That was certainly true of me. But try I did.

For about eight years I was the last ditch effort before the divorce attorney. Ted started doing more with his wife and children. A couple of times a week, there might be an actual conversation. He found some activities to share with his wife. For example, they enjoyed walking to a neighborhood restaurant for supper. He realized that he could joke with the kids if he e-mailed them. This opened up a tolerable amount of interaction, and Ted started enjoying getting to know them. Things plodded along until the roof fell in.

He was caught buying pot from one of his own students.

The police were incredibly cooperative and the legal system bent for him. He was forced to resign from his teaching job and sign himself into the psychiatric unit of a hospital in a neighboring town. This hospital had a new PTSD program and was renowned for their drug treatment center. For someone who seemed like he'd lost everything, the truth was, he was about to reinvent himself in a new, stable, much more healed way.

This was the tipping point for Ted, the moment when he knew it was time to make a significant change. He had been in therapy on and off for almost twenty-five years, both in veterans' programs and in private practices. He had seen his wife and children slip away as he slipped further and further inside himself. Now his family was about to leave him. Those well-constructed defenses were going to have to be dismantled.

His Signs

Isolation was Ted's main defense mechanism. Since he couldn't trust himself to let down his walls in any way, he did everything in his power to stay behind a tight defensive shield of civility and information. As long as he was using the part of his brain where information was stored, he was fine. He could teach, give directions, read, work on crossword puzzles and Sudokus, but God forbid he be asked something personal or expected to engage in an intimate exchange. Isolation was the way he handled his great fear that he would fall apart, start blubbering, scream his nightmares out loud, strangle someone who challenged him or even punch the next guy or girl who tried to talk to him on an emotional level.

I remember one time Ted came into therapy and I waited for him to say something. I waited for an entire hour. Neither of us said one word. It's much more usual that I hardly have the door shut before a client starts talking, and sometimes I have a hard time speaking a word. But silence? I could only hope it was therapeutic in some way.

The isolation from those he lived with and loved was, of course, devastating isolation for Ted as well as his family. He so feared himself and his reactions, was so terror-stricken by what he had done in Viet Nam, so disgusted by what he had seen and smelled and heard and felt, that he was sure if he let his defenses down in any way, he would go back there. He had awoken, back in the days when he was still trying to sleep with his wife, to find himself shaking her, and she wide-eyed and hoarse from screaming.

He had never chanced falling asleep with one of the babies

in his arms, because he just couldn't trust what he might do. How poignant that the actions which were intended to keep his family safe from him had made them fear him. How sad that his valiant and gallant service to his country had ruined his chances to serve his own wife and children in any meaningful way.

The fear and terror which plagued Ted were barely reduced by his pot consumption. It might be more accurate to say that his pot smoking allowed him to breathe without sounding like a freight train and without feeling constantly like he had to outrun one. His running provided nature's most effective natural anti-depressant. It was inadequate for him to walk or jog or run a few miles. He became a marathoner. Unfortunately, Ted was quickly addicted to both the pot and the running. We generally consider exercise of almost any form, no matter how compulsive or consuming, to be a benign addiction. You may be "addicted" to it, in that you may have to do it on a regular basis and for a prescribed amount of time and you may feel sick and unable to concentrate until you do it, but it is not really harmful. Actually, it's more like a habit.

Pot, at least in the amount and frequency Ted used, was definitely a harmful addiction. The cost to him and his family was astronomical in every way. Pot reduces anxiety. But then when the anxiety comes back, it comes back at an infinitesimally higher level. The more you use, the more you need to use and the more quickly you need to re-use. Pot also interferes with ambition and drive. When Ted came home from the university at night, he was done in. He had no remaining energy for himself, his family, his community or even the cat.

But the addiction continued and built as did Ted's dependence on cigarettes. He was smoking, both nicotine and marijuana, in an attempt to turn his brain off, in an attempt to calm down, to numb out. The running, actually, did the same thing for him. Cigarettes, pot and running all helped Ted to lose his mind or at least the constant mind chatter. The saying "Lose your mind to keep your sanity" certainly applied to Ted.

Ted had been wounded in Viet Nam and lived in constant physical pain. His legs and back had endured surgery after surgery. He was in a VA hospital for the first eighteen months that he was back in the States. The extensive physical and psychological therapy had him walking without a limp and functioning in society. What remained was pain. The pain, like everything else in his body, his memories, his senses, his anxiety, just couldn't be quiet. Nag, nag, nag. When I met Ted, twenty years later, he was suffering most from shoulder and neck pain. They were not the primary pain from the injuries, but they were the residual pain. Ted was stiff-necked and carrying the weight of the world on his shoulders.

In <u>War and the Soul</u> Ed Tick tells the story of a soldier who explained that in the most fearsome and most terrorizing moments of his life, his soul fled. It ran. It saved itself. It separated itself from his body. The soldier told Dr. Tick that his soul was right there beside him. But it refused to climb back inside. Too dangerous there. Ted said the same thing. His soul was gone. Invisible. No longer a part of him. What soul? He had lost his soul. He had therefore lost his connection and his ability to ever connect to God. He was soulless and godless. He was the walking dead. He was . . . Empty.

His Steps

It would be impossible to say what Ted's first step was. He was so deeply in denial that learning to recognize himself as a PTSD survivor might have been our first challenge. Ted was from the in-between generation who believed they should have just been able to go to war and come home and fit right back into their former lives. Except that NOTHING from their former lives fit any more.

Ted knew he was different, felt he didn't belong, and carried the additional burden of having been a hero in a war which was considered by a large segment of the population to have been un-heroic. What in World War II and the Korean War had been a given, that the men and women who returned were entitled to the highest regard and the deepest loyalty, was not true in this war. As always with society's big changes and gradual awarenesses, this was not comfortable, not expected, not pretty and not nice. Protesters lined the streets and the alleys and were at the initial stages of this new wisdom unable to draw the distinction between supporting the war and supporting our troops. We've corrected this imbalance. Unfortunately, an entire generation of soldiers has suffered because of our blindness and lack of empathy.

Ted had experienced almost twenty years of on and off therapy through the Veteran's Administration before he found himself in private therapy. I had seen his wife as a client and quickly realized I wasn't going to make much progress with her until we brought him into therapy, too. When she told him she was "done," he decided it couldn't hurt anything.

His wife relayed that Ted was most frequently "absent" from life and that she and the children could never count on him in any way to be there for them. He quickly agreed. He went "away." He went "inside." He was "gone." The why was immediately evident.

How to change the coping mechanism to something all could endure was much harder.

Ted and his wife had developed a strong, unswerving pattern. He went "away." She got mad and wouldn't talk to him, wouldn't have sex with him and pretended he didn't exist. When she got mad at him, wouldn't have sex with him, pretended he didn't exist, he went further inside. Her anger and his shame created a self-sustaining see-saw. The more she got angry, the more he receded. The more he receded, the angrier and more rejecting she became.

My background in systems theory helped me to explain to Ted and Tess just what their negative self-supporting pattern was and why we needed to break it. They were both bright enough and determined enough to understand that we were fighting something big. When Ted distanced, Tess needed to stay available. When she got mad and frigid and blaming, he needed to stay present. They had to stop reacting and simply keep on, as they say in Alcoholics Anonymous, "doing the next right thing." They had to continue acting in love, even when they believed the other was withdrawing love. What a challenging assignment. Actually, everyone to whom I have ever given this assignment has had a very difficult time with it. Too bad. Miracles could be had with this one simple awareness.

To his credit, Ted was willing to engage in therapy. We started talking about his childhood, which meant we were laying the ground work for, as they now phrase it, his adverse childhood experiences. It is important for PTSD survivors to trace the stress as far back as possible. Priceless compassion and understanding for the self come with the realization that as a child one was helpless and victimized. Ted started remembering that he was taunted and teased when he was a boy and was made to feel "less than" and "weak" and "inadequate." This was the framework from which he went into war.

In therapy he started drawing, journaling, talking, both intellectually and emotionally, and admitting that he felt different from most people. He admitted that he felt anxious all the time and that his mind never shut off. He admitted that he ached constantly, physically and emotionally. He admitted that he felt powerless and defensive when his wife or children or anyone else confronted him or asked him why he did what he did or felt like he felt.

For as long as I knew him as a client (we have since become colleagues), I would ask him, "How's your soul?" It was as though I was always trying to reach the soulful part of him and never could. After reading Edward Tick's War and the Soul both Ted and I realized that his soul, too, had fled in Viet Nam. His soul, however, didn't stay beside him, as did the soldier's in the story. His soul hid out-of-sight behind his back. It, too, ran from feelings of abject terror. He knows, now, when it fled and has written a poem about that moment.

> Her eyes red, glowing
> Her village napped to kindling;
> Side show to the war.

He had been in charge and had given the order to napalm the village. The day before an elderly woman had fed him in her hooch. That evening the enemy tripped the ambush that had been set for them and the village was ordered destroyed. When Ted and his men returned to the village after it had been leveled, hers was the first body they saw. Her eyes, red, glowing haunted his sleep for the next thirty years.

And there were other moments of unbearable terror. Another description in Haiku:

> Rockets exploding.
> Glued to a hospital bed
> Never sane again.

Ever notice that the words "scared" and "scarred" are so similar? Be scared and add an "r." Sometimes we're "scared out of our wits." Sometimes we're "scared to death." Anytime we are terrorized, I believe we are traumatized. What happens in our body short-circuits our electrical system. We have, in effect, a near death experience. If we were cats, we would have used up one of our lives. Terror becomes trauma and being scared results in being scarred. Both result in our shutting down.

The recent experience of another patient offers insight into Ted's dissociation. She was attempting to deal with an old terror, a time when she had shut down on herself. It was many years previous. In therapy, trying to access these distant memories, she dissociated. She simply left. She recognized nothing from her present life, including her daughter who was in the waiting room. She had no idea who she was. She was taken to the hospital and given every test imaginable. Slowly, as the hours passed, with her terrified daughter watching and praying, she came back to inhabit her own body. Fascinatingly, she remembers nothing about that missing period of time or all the tests she underwent.

It is from incidents like this that I get my great respect for the conscious and unconscious mind. If we are not conscious of something, I think it is better not to dig. Our entire make-up, our whole being, is programmed for survival and anything we do to disrupt survival--like remembering things too horrendous to remember--will put us in a precarious position. Some things we aren't supposed to remember, or we would. This was my understanding. I have to admit that in Ted's case I was wrong.

The psychiatric unit Ted entered following his arrest was using a form of immersion therapy. I personally believe this to be theoretically dangerous, as I just explained when relating the account of the woman with the strange amnesia. Immersing someone back into their trauma takes the risk that they will become psychically stuck there and never re-emerge. I have the same problem with hypnosis, by the way. I'm not sure that we should try to trick the unconscious mind into telling us things the conscious mind has rejected and eliminated. Having professed my cautions about such dangerous, risky treatment protocols, let me tell you how well it worked for Ted. It provided his breakthrough.

Ted was instructed to tell in exquisite detail his terrifying and traumatizing experiences in Viet Nam. He talked for two hours. Then he was sent home with the two hours of tapes and told to listen to his own voice recounting these experiences morning, afternoon and evening. Within a week it had lost its power over him.

Ted started attending NA meetings (Narcotics Anonymous) and progressed from participant to leader in a number of months. He started attending a Viet Nam veterans' group and became involved in workshops, retreats, and poetry writing classes. He volunteers twenty hours a week at the psychiatric hospital that gave him a chance to reclaim his life.

Ted is happier than I've ever seen him. He has re-invented himself and re-created his life purpose. He is busy every day with meaningful projects and his volunteer activities. As fellow counselors, we send each other articles and news of upcoming retreats and resources. He is helping me learn about the veterans PTSD community and I am helping him to become part of the mental health establishment.

My Story

At some point I saw every member of Ted's immediate family as clients. I found each to be a bright, talented, determined member of society. The children, like their parents, are highly educated, each holding at least one graduate degree. They are each compassionate. Every one of them has been touched and altered in some way by Ted's PTSD. What is remarkable about his children's reactions is that they are using their father's experiences to direct and deepen their own lives. Perhaps this is because they have forgiven him and embrace his recovery, a process shared by the children of many veterans.

Tess's story is different. She remains the most wounded one in the family. Having held herself and her family together when Ted was unavailable, Tess has now folded in on herself, agoraphobic and uninterested in anything that does not involve her children. She seems to feel, simply put, betrayed by her husband. She had married someone very different than the man who came home from Viet Nam.

As a group they illustrate that PTSD is a family affair. When one family member suffers, everyone feels the ripples. It seems that Ted's children were typical in that, like the children of so many other wounded warriors, they were able to forgive and accept. Tess, too, was typical in that like many wives of veterans, it was she who was the most deeply affected and the most fundamentally betrayed. These women married big, tough soldiers who were going to protect and adore them. After the war they found themselves in charge and, like Tess, had a stranger living in the attic or basement. The stranger was emotionally unavailable, physically shattered, mentally preoccupied and spiritually dead. Not what they had married. Not the contract they had signed.

Ted, like many or even most veterans, did and does love his wife. The problem is not about his feelings or about any change in those feelings. It is very hard for someone who is going down for the third time to worry about taking out the trash. His wounds made it impossible for him to do right by her. I remember twenty years ago asking her if she would be "done" with him had he come home from Viet Nam without arms and been unable to embrace her physically. She answered that he would have had no choice about that. She felt and feels to this day that he had choices about the way he suffered from PTSD and the way he made his family suffer. I have to believe it is the mental health community which has failed them all. I also choose to believe we are getting much wiser.

Tess's reaction demonstrates a very poignant aspect of PTSD. You can't see it.

No one can see PTSD. No one can see who has PTSD. Those with PTSD suffer in silence and are invisible.

No one can see PTSD. No one can see who has PTSD.

Many mental illness issues, like PTSD, since they are not visible, unlike a broken leg or the effects of an amputation, are considered to be matters of willpower and discipline. For example, many people believe they would never be depressed. They'd just pull themselves up by the bootstraps. They would never suffer from anxiety. They'd just take a deep breath and calm themselves down. They'd never have problems no matter what happened in their childhoods or what happened to them in Viet Nam or Iraq or during Hurricane Katrina or anything else. THEY are strong. People who are affected by mental health issues are weak.

What an unenlightened and uninformed position. To follow that reasoning, good drivers never have accidents and good people never get divorced. On and on we go with our judgments and our condemnations. The obese are all gluttons and the poor are all lazy and the unkempt are all slobs. A recent example of this was a woman who came in with postpartum depression. Her husband had said to her. "How can you be depressed? You have a new baby. You told me you wanted this baby." Oh, so her desire for this baby was supposed to be stronger than any chemical and hormonal changes inside her body and mind? Was she weak to have admitted that she felt something different from what society determined she should have felt?

Was Ted weak when he came back from Viet Nam with PTSD?

Was Tess weak when she was truly, finally "done"?

We simply and truly cannot judge any of this. We cannot say, "Oh, I would have done this differently and that differently." You would have? Who knows, because you weren't in it. It wasn't your path. We are born with a certain chemical make-up and raised in a certain environment and pushed and pulled to believe and think certain things. The Native Americans understood that until we walk in someone else's moccasins, we just can't know. We just can't understand. If only we would realize that we just cannot judge.

> *"Before you criticize someone, walk a mile in her moccasins. That way when you do criticize that person you'll be a mile away and you'll have her moccasins."*
>
> **The Wisdom of Grey Owl**

Memories

It's been a long time, almost forty years.

Dark nights followed by even darker days.

Jack, Tom, Henry, Bill, John.

Each gone.

Their faces forever etched in the mirrors of my mind.

It's been a long time.

Jack, whose life ended with the explosion of a land mine.

Tom, the same, only days before rotating home.

Henry and Bill, each taken by friendly fire,

A short round before either had time to react.

And John killed instantly by an AK-47 round to his heart

While crawling across a rice paddy.

It's been a long time.

Woeful women wounded by eyeless bullets during fearsome firefights.

Charred children burned beyond belief by napalm.

There are many truisms in life.

One, originating during the turbulent 60's read,

"War is not healthy for children and other living things."

Add to that,

"Sorry sights seen in combat remain locked in the mind forever."

Maggie

Her Story

     Maggie's story began for me years before I ever met Maggie. Her dad had been a student of mine when I taught at a Midwestern university. I remembered him and I liked him. Adam was, in fact, the kind of student every college professor loves: an adult, a husband, a father, a successful businessman. He was in college to learn and to earn a degree. He never missed a class, had every assignment done on time and to the letter, and he made friends with other students, not just the smart or popular ones. He liked everyone, and everyone liked him. He owned a well-respected catering business and frequently came to class with cookies or sandwiches or something that he professed would go to waste if we didn't all help out by eating them.

     When class was over and his well-earned A was history, Adam would show up during my office hours with two cups of coffee and something for me to take home to my family. The something was usually some delectable food he was experimenting with or sometimes tickets to a local event. He'd hang out for a few minutes and talk and then take off. He never overstayed his welcome, nor did he ever overstep any boundaries.

     I did learn during these visits that Adam had an unhappy marriage but two daughters he adored. The older girl was the golden child. The younger was a screw-up and a cold fish. Since she was a baby, he told me, Maggie had hated to be held and touched. She'd stiffen when anyone picked her up. We brainstormed a little on how to help this child, and then, slowly, Adam disappeared from my life.

     After I had transitioned completely from teacher to therapist, I got a phone call from him. Maggie had just turned eighteen and Adam wondered if I'd see her as a client. She was confused about what to do after high school. Oh, and also, she had run away from home and was staying with a girlfriend's family. Adam was enlisting my help to get her back home.

     I've provided this introduction of Maggie because I want you to share my incredulity when she comes into my office and tells me her story. The reason she even agreed to come was tied to the fact that she had a car for which her dad made the payments and bought the gas. Coming to see me was the price for keeping and driving the car.

Maggie was a hard shell of a girl, petite, blonde, blue-eyed and frighteningly thin. She wore no makeup and no smile. She was dwarfed inside her clothes. The first promise she extracted from me was in response to a threat. If I ever told her father anything, she said, she'd stop coming. She was over eighteen, I assured her. As long as she wasn't planning to kill him or herself, or anyone else for that matter, anything she told me was strictly between us.

It still took Maggie a few weeks and a few tests of me before she trusted me enough to get down to business. First, she told me about Barbara, the golden girl. Barbara was at a prestigious east coast college studying pre-med. Barbara was perfect. She was the high school valedictorian. Maggie was getting one of those high school diplomas which admitted merely that you'd attended school. She joked that Barbara was the "good twin" and she was the "evil twin," even though they weren't twins.

Then Maggie told me about her mother. Her mother detested her, criticized her, told her she wished Maggie had never been born and knew that Maggie was a conniving bitch. She would warn any man Maggie brought home never to marry her. Her mother absolutely, positively hated Maggie. Maggie could remember no happy moments. None.

Then we talked about the wonderful, loving grandma, her father's mother, and the dirty old man who was her grandfather. She said that her grandfather was constantly trying to stick his tongue in her mouth. She remembered sitting on his lap as a little girl and feeling his erect penis against her bottom. Everyone in the room was acting like all was well as tears slid down her face. She remembers her grandma bringing her a cookie so she'd stop crying. No one thought to remove her from grandpa's lap.

Maggie adored her grandma, but every time she went to visit she had to outwit and outmaneuver her grandfather. Luckily, she added casually, she didn't even remember all the things he had tried, and she had no idea how many had been successful before she became clever enough to start eluding him. Maggie added that Barbara, the golden child, would have nothing to do with the grandparents, which upset her father, so it was a chance for Maggie to shine if she succumbed and went to see them.

Maggie was one of a handful of clients I've had over the years who has been unable to tolerate sitting for the therapeutic hour, actually about fifty minutes. She'd sit for a while and then get up and walk around and then sit back down. I asked her if she thought she was anxious. "Oh, sure," she answered. "I'm on Xanax for the anxiety."

She had acquaintances, she reported, but no friends. She partied with lots of different people. Just pot and beer, she assured me. We talked about the pot being illegal and she being underage for legal drinking. They were all careful, she insisted. And so what if they got caught? Their parents all knew. It was their parents who bought them the beer.

"Your dad buys you beer?" I asked.

"Sure."

It finally occurred to me to say, "So, let's talk about your dad."

"My father has sexually abused me as far back as I can remember, and he continues to rape me to this day, which is why I'm not living at home." She said all this in a voice devoid of emotion.

I sat stunned.

I've encountered this dichotomy before, but it had never before been personal. This perpetrator was a man I liked and admired. He had hugged me and we had laughed together. He had always been completely appropriate and totally respectful. I would have trusted my children with this man. I thought I knew him. I wondered how many other people had trusted this baseball coach and Sunday schoolteacher.

It is not uncommon for pedophiles to be attractive and charming. For some, it is how they lure their prey. It is also not uncommon for those who abuse children to have a snow-white cover. The dad who climbed the stairs and then went either left or right to rape one of his daughters was a church deacon. We've all read about priests and ministers who have harmed those under their protection. But this was someone whose cover I had bought.

I'm sure I sat and stared at Maggie for an interminable amount of time. My mind couldn't find any words to send to my mouth. And then I remember saying to her, "Maggie, I am so dreadfully, horribly sorry. That is so reprehensible. I hope you know there is nothing you ever did to make that happen. That is all him, Maggie. He's the adult. You're the child." And then it hit me. That bastard had waited until she was eighteen to send her into therapy. Had she still been underage, I could have called Children's Services and they could have investigated and prosecuted. Now, at eighteen, it was up to her.

Maggie would need to prosecute this man who had sexually abused her all her life with the despicable help of her mother's complicit, critical hatred, her sister's inexplicably, untouchable exclusion from the abuse, her grandfather's lecherous abuse of his own, and her grandmother's benign, stupid, inexcusable neglect. Yeah. That seemed like a great plan. Dad had everyone on the dole, even Maggie. Who was going to blow that whistle? Plus, he was Mr. Congeniality. Who'd believe the evil twin?

Maggie stayed out of the house and came to therapy religiously. She appreciated the irony of Adam's paying for what she was saying. She worked at this job and that and tried to get her head on straight. It was like watching someone swim in wet cement. Then her grandmother died, and that seemed to free her. She announced she had joined the Army. She was leaving for boot camp. I was half thrilled, half terrified. Maggie hated authority, had lost a couple jobs because the bosses were jerks, and she was still a painfully thin, painfully vulnerable little girl. She just happened to be twenty-one. I wasn't sure I could trust the United States Army to protect her.

We wrote letters back and forth during the two years Maggie was away. I encouraged and supported her in every way I could. And then she was back. She went back on dad's paycheck but not back to his bed. She found a job in a nursing home that she really liked. She called to tell me this news and to say that she'd make an appointment soon. She was ready to start really putting some work into therapy. It seemed as if she had finally turned the corner and there might be some light in her future. I imagined briefly that this was Maggie's tipping point, her chance to get down to it and recreate herself. A chance to begin healing. I was to find out that that was not so. Not for Maggie.

Her Signs

Her anxiety was the worst symptom she displayed. Maggie's mind would simply not settle down and neither would her body. The chemical rushes inside this poor girl played havoc with her concentration and her focus. I wondered if she had attention deficit disorder and would have investigated that had time permitted. She was a bright young woman, but she could never slow down enough to pay attention. She was rarely in the present, always watching the radar for potential disasters. It was a lesson that she had learned well because of her parents.

Drugs, Xanax in particular, were Maggie's major coping mechanism and self-soothing technique. When I asked her how much Xanax she was prescribed, she told me one milligram. That's a powerful prescription. Many people take .25 or .50 milligrams and sometimes cut the pills in halves or quarters. It slowly came out that she had Xanax prescriptions from more than one doctor which she had filled at more than one pharmacy. The cold truth of the matter: Maggie was addicted to Xanax. At her highest level of consumption, she was taking thirty-one pills a day. Obviously, she'd run out before her prescriptions were due to be refilled. Then she would do whatever she had to do to get more. Xanax is available on the street for either money or sex. Maggie paid with both.

Maggie was an adrenalin junkie, too. She simply couldn't get enough thrills to calm her down. Promiscuity, random partying, going home with different guys she had just met to places she had never been to engage in things she would be coerced to try, like homemade pornography tapes, were simply a part of life for Maggie. She sought danger constantly and she sought new and more challenging highs. She drove frequently while under the influence. In the time I knew her she totaled three cars and walked away from each accident. Thankfully, she never hurt anyone else in her thoughtless and compulsive search for thrills.

Maggie had no boyfriend ever in her life. She had no girlfriend either. She seemed not to care whether she had sex with a man, multiple men, a woman, or some combination. She had Alan's confusion about sexual preference, but she didn't have his restraint about experimenting. She had a first abortion at fifteen, a second at twenty. The last time I heard from Maggie, she told me she would get the results of an AIDS test the following week. I never knew what the test showed, and neither did she.

Maggie hated her life and hated herself. She was careless because she could care less. She walked out on people who tried to help her, walked away from promising jobs and deserted anyone who got too close. I walked on egg shells. She finally left me, but not by her own choice.

Her Steps

Maggie tried something that not too many of my clients have tried. She moved. If we cannot figure out how to distance ourselves from toxic people emotionally, by setting boundaries and establishing our own empowered control, the next best thing to do is to distance ourselves physically. Move. Move out of town, out of state, out of the country, if need be. Maggie had no where to go and no one with whom to go, so she enlisted in the Army. It was a guarantee for movement.

When I meet a new client for the first time, I always do a genogram. This is a picture of a client's family of origin, including parents and grandparents and, if the client is married, the parents and grandparents of the spouse. When I get to siblings, I'm always amused to find that this brother is in California and this brother lives in Louisiana and this sister settled in Wisconsin and my client is still here with the toxic parents. I always want to say, "That's why you're the client and they're enjoying a phone call home every Sunday evening from 8:00 - 8:15." Wyoming, I'm always suggesting. Or, go west. Or south. They always have excuses, typically jobs and kids in school. See, that's what happens when you're the responsible one.

My mother was the responsible one. She took her mother and her sister into her home and her brothers headed for California. Literally. And then, when the boys came home, they were greeted with ticker tape parades and my mother got to cook for everybody. My dad was usually allowed to buy the food and take out the garbage. Both of my parents were resentful. But they were stuck with their responsible personalities. Having such parents has made it possible for me to understand people acting out of responsibility. It's always the good stewards, the loyal, dedicated ones who stick it out and try to learn to move emotionally, since their consciences won't let them desert the ship. (Please understand, those who move do nothing wrong. They are not morally inferior. They simply prioritize their lives differently.)

Maggie wasn't the responsible type. She got out of Dodge. Unfortunately, she returned to Dodge. The toxicity she left behind had fermented while she was gone and turned more toxic still. Moving had been a good idea for her. She was simply ill-equipped to make it on her own. She had no coping skills except endurance and no way to self-soothe except Xanax. We were working on both, but it was too little too late.

Maggie tried to tune down her self-medicating and work with her addiction. Although she realized she was addicted, she wouldn't join Narcotics Anonymous or go into rehab. She simply stopped taking drugs and went cold turkey when she enlisted in the Army. That lasted for six months. And then life got too tough. She had substituted exercise and pushing her body and building her strength in boot camp. Then she was given an office job with a lot of time on her hands and the need to face the anxiety of never being able to concentrate. She went back to the tried and true. She somehow managed an honorable discharge while addicted to the pills. I'll never know how.

She tried therapy, of course, and she did learn to trust me somewhat as I proved myself over time. Our letter writing helped, since it was clearly not something I had to do and showed her I really did care for her and about her. I do believe she would have come back to therapy. I am unconvinced that it would have been much help, but she could have had an ally and someone who believed her.

Ultimately, Maggie fell into that conundrum where one has a choice of being either bad or stupid. Bad or uncooperative. Bad or unable. Bad or incapable. I think this is why so many kids in school are "bad." It's preferable to admitting they can't read, can't calm their brains down enough to think, or can't pass a test. Perhaps the letters of the words swim or the letters of the words reverse themselves or the words on the page don't make sense in their heads. What kid is going to admit something like this? I'd rather be bad. My other choice is to admit that I have been so wounded and tarnished that I cannot pass among the civilized and seem like one of them. "I choose bad. I am a bad girl. What are you going do about it?" I can almost hear Maggie saying the words.

My Story

Maggie had to be included in this book because her story was such a learning curve for me. Over and over my thoughts of her remind me that things are not what they seem. Perpetrators do not have a certain look or a certain smell and they may be your best friends or your husband or your neighbor or the soccer coach or the gym teacher, even the therapist. Knowing that I could not rely on my own intuition, my own education, my own powers of observation was a painful lesson. Now, when people like my daughter-in-law suspect everyone, I admit that she has a point. We simply cannot tell. And I don't believe this has changed over the centuries. I think it has always been so. The good and the not-so-good or even the downright evil pass on the street and tip their hats or smile sweetly and even seductively at each other. We cannot know. This is one of life's greatest anxieties. Those who were abused as children, who endured what are now called "adverse childhood experiences," learned early what those of us whose parents protected us must come to learn late. Things are not what they seem.

The adverse childhood experiences (ACE) study is available online at "http://www.acestudy.org/". This study delineates children who grew up with any of the following household dysfunctions: substance abuse, parental separation and divorce, mental illness, battered mothers, or criminal behavior. Children who suffered psychological, physical or sexual abuse and emotional or physical neglect were included, obviously, in the group of children who endured adverse childhood experiences. Such experiences were predictive of obesity, attempted suicide, depression, violent victimization, victimization of domestic violence, drug abuse, HIV risk, smoking and lung disease, ischemic heart disease, adolescent illnesses, reproductive illnesses, alcohol abuse, dangerous sexual behavior, the instability of relationships, homelessness, and poor performance in the workplace. See the link for much more on this.

Maggie could have been the poster child for adverse childhood experiences. She endured it all. And she suffered so profoundly because of it. When I think about Maggie now, only The Serenity Prayer gives me any peace.

I couldn't help her. I didn't like the feeling. I didn't like the powerlessness. I also didn't like the realization that I couldn't change what had happened to her. I couldn't forgive her father for what he had done and for the lie he was living and promoting, and I hated her mother for betraying all of us as mothers with our inherent obligation and privilege to protect, in the womb and beyond. I had then and have had since a difficult time finding serenity when I think of Maggie. Typically, I feel like saddling Silver and whistling for Tonto and setting off to avenge the wrongs.

> *God, grant me the serenity to*
>
> *Accept the things I cannot change*
>
> *Courage to change those things I can*
>
> *And wisdom to know the difference.*

It is a very profound Buddhist learning to know that injustice exists and I must open my heart and mind and let things flow as they will.

There is no closure in this case. There is no way to ever let go because there are unanswered questions and unquestioned answers. Maggie, at the age of twenty-three, was on her way to work at the nursing home early one morning when she passed a slow moving vehicle on a hill and rammed head first into a garbage truck. She was killed instantly. Was she under the influence of her Xanax? Did she mean to die that spring morning or was it, as the police ruled it to be, an accident? And how do we accept that this child never had a chance in life? How do I accept what I cannot change?

I guess for me the answer which has slowly evolved is to do in Maggie's honor what I can for everyone else who enters my realm of being. To silently dedicate to Maggie my efforts, my awareness, and my belief. Because she never had a chance, I try to constantly recommit myself to helping the new Maggies, the girls and guys and women and men, who come in battered and feeling crazy, to as much serenity as I can muster on any given day.

William

His Story

Spiritual leaders of diverse groups often wonder if we choose our parents. Perhaps, they suggest, we select parents who will nurture us or challenge us or even beat us up if we feel we need to be beaten. The theory is that we choose parents who will provide for us, either positively or negatively, what our souls most need to advance through our karmic or developmental path. I am not suggesting whether this is true or not true. But, when you meet someone like William, if you have ever heard this theory, you surely wonder if this was William's preference.

William was born to a sixteen-year-old, red-headed sophomore beauty who had a brief sexual fling with a twenty-three year old African-American law student. The red-headed child never told her beau that she was pregnant. She simply had the baby and immediately gave him over for adoption. I would guess this sixteen year old felt the need to preserve her figure. Her baby boy was born with bowed legs and club feet, having been rather confined in a rather tight space. She named him Robert and requested he go to a family where a college education would be a possibility.

A foster mom took him home from the hospital and almost immediately took him everywhere she went, including to the bowling alley. She performed the exercises needed to reshape his squashed legs and feet, named him Justin, and loved him up for four months while she introduced him to strikes and spares and sustained loud noises.

Then adoptive parents appeared and William went home with two liberal, white, hippie, college professors who already had a biological child but believed that adoption was the right thing to do. They never imagined that this baby's cocoa-colored skin might prove to be a problem, for them or for the baby. After all, it was 1974. The decade of racial unrest was over. Another biological child came two years later to complete this family. And William, with his third name in four months, grew up as a bi-racial, adopted son sandwiched between two white biological children.

William almost immediately proved himself to be different from his two siblings, not only because, as his older sibling noticed at four, William was "the tan man." While his siblings were quiet,

William talked a blue streak. While they were cautious, William was impetuous. While they obeyed the rules, William never bothered to learn the rules. He threw his first party when he was in fifth grade. He and his friends, male and female, skipped school and hung out at William's house one winter day while his parents were at the university teaching.

William's predisposition to danger and adventure deepened when he was fifteen and fell in love with a fifteen-year-old Caucasian girl. Her parents forbid the friendship, admitting it was because of his mixed race, and William started a painful journey to find out who he was and where he belonged.

When he was with his black friends, other blacks called him Uncle Tom. When he was with his white friends, other whites called him a nigger and called his friends nigger lovers. Everyone who knew him as an individual liked him. He was a four point student and an incredibly talented athlete, but in the mid-eighties society had no place for him. When at eighteen he married a white girl, dropping out of the college his biological mother had dreamed of for him, William and his new wife watched in horror what happened to other mixed couples in their neighborhood.

Before his marriage there were run-ins with the law and run-ins with drugs and alcohol. After his marriage there was only work and an increasing number of children to support. He and his wife had agreed, when he dropped out of college, that she would start college and get her degree and then it would be his turn. After fifteen years of marriage, she had more than enough credits to graduate but had never done so, and his turn had never come.

In one of his many attempts to support his family, he decided to join the Reserves. Soon after he did, he was sent to Iraq. There the traumas of his childhood, not fitting in, being different, not being accepted, loving danger and adventure, all crystallized on a lonely rooftop watching the bombs explode near-by and keeping vigilant while his soldier brothers slept. He was sent with a gun he had been inadequately trained to use, and with not enough supplies and not the right supplies. His family and friends sent care package after care package, with everything from fans to long woolen underwear to flea collars to keep sand fleas at bay.

William describes his time in Iraq as a turning point, but he wasn't to realize it for a while. First he came home on a medical discharge, with nerve damage on his right side which would give him chronic pain. Then he fought his wife, who hadn't wanted him to enlist in the first place, and then he fought the alcohol which had dulled her criticism, quieted the bombs of his memory and numbed some of the chronic pain.

William is now a divorced dad, running a house, raising his children, drinking non-alcoholic beer, working his day job and getting a 3.8 at college. He plans to be a counselor for other vets. He is happier than he has been since early childhood, has his head screwed on fairly straight and is focused on his present fathering and his future career.

His Signs

From the time he was a baby, William couldn't sleep. His mom tells of his awakening eight, ten times a night. She would reach down in his crib and pat his back, and he'd go right back to sleep. This went on until he was about fourteen months old at which time she begged the pediatrician to drug one of them so they could sleep through the night. Two nights of cough syrup with codeine and William was sleeping. But throughout his life, the slightest disruption or stress, and he went back to his hyper-vigilant state of insomnia.

His anxiety, as in most male children, looked like ADHD and sent him seeking adrenalin. At two he reports being lost and his mom finding him on top of the refrigerator, sitting still and smiling at her while she called and searched. At fourteen he took the family car for a spin one day when everyone was out. He was the star of every team he was on, playing harder than most people worked. At eighteen he was already on the university football team when he decided to get married instead. He had sex early, drank early and often and tried every substance offered him. Cigarettes were a long time addiction, until, as with the alcohol, he stopped cold turkey and never started again. All of these adrenalin rushes and addictions were aimed at reducing his anxiety.

Some of the ways we might know if we are adrenalin junkies:

Schedule ourselves into oblivion

Be constantly late for things

Experiment with drugs

Consume massive amounts of alcohol
Seek and promote drama

Engage in risky behaviors

Isolation was an indicator that William wasn't doing well. He had months, after he was first home from the war, when he would get up and go to work and other than that, spend his days and nights in his room. This sounds like Ted, doesn't it? William and Ted and a million suffering others. He would avoid his wife and children as well as his family and friends. He definitely suffered from impaired volition, as this usual go-getter collapsed in on himself. His life-long coping mechanism of compulsive busyness had failed him.

Of all his PTSD symptoms, surely the most troublesome for William always has been and probably always will be that he cannot shut off his mind. He thinks and analyzes and plans and self-criticizes and worries and frets constantly. He has trouble concentrating and focusing and when he does get zeroed in on something, he tends to obsess.

His Steps

William tried responsibility. Unwittingly, but nonetheless consistently, William made himself as responsible to others as he possibly could, thereby giving himself a reason to work against his more natural predisposition of irresponsibility and impetuousness. As a child, he became a leader. Whether it was scouting, social interaction, an art class or his ever present sports, he stepped to the front of the pack and took the lead. He dropped out of college to be responsible for a young, single woman and her baby. They had other children and he worked more jobs and welcomed responsibility in all areas of his life.

Responsibility led to purpose, whether it was as father, construction site boss, church deacon or baseball coach. Indeed, William kept himself in a whirlwind of compulsive busyness, but he also scripted his life with purpose and responsibility. He made himself accountable for the welfare and safety of others. He kept himself as well and safe as possible almost by default. He was the leader in many things, and the leader needs to lead by example.

He has always joked that fear is a very powerful motivator for him, and so when he had a very scary experience with alcohol, he quit cold turkey. After he had that pretty well handled, he decided to quit cigarettes the same way. Pain medication followed those first two addictions, and that, too, he left behind. His tendency to be a black and white thinker has definitely caused him some problems, but when it came to leaving his addictions in the past, it served him well. William simply made up his mind that he wasn't going to be addicted to anything.

While this transition was underway, William tried physical therapy and found that some of the very simple therapy techniques could do more for his constant pain than popping the pain pills, and without the numbing effect on his mind and spirit. When the pain was under more control, he started running. Of course, a fellow like William wouldn't start walking. He is now running marathons. Mind over matter again. As Carl Jung says, "Our greatest strengths are our greatest weaknesses." Consequently, our greatest weaknesses are our greatest strengths, too.

> *Our greatest strengths are our greatest weaknesses.*
>
> *Our greatest weaknesses are our greatest strengths.*
>
> *Carl Jung*

At the foundation of all these steps was the first step William took when he was released from Walter Reed Hospital. He sought out the local Veterans Administration counseling center and became a client. His counselor, who he's been seeing on and off for almost five years, was a major influence in his life, talking him through many of his fears as well as leading him to value who he is and to dream of who he will become.

At a local university William found a veterans program based on the platoon model. A group of former soldiers enter college together and they help each other to succeed in the classes they take together and to encourage each other in their lives. This is not a structured group, simply a group of like minded souls doing similar things at the same time. They just naturally are supportive of each other. So, William, in his thirties, is a college student determined to be a responsible and productive member of society, using his talents and experiences to help himself as well as others.

William has chosen not to join AA or NA or a soldiers group. His steps have been personal ones and, as we've seen throughout this book of case studies, one size does not fit all. I remember reading somewhere that the PTSD treatments which work best are those where the survivor becomes the author of his or her own story, the general contractor of his or her new, improved psychic house. Each of us must pick and choose from the available list of steps and possible healing tools, those which most speak to our story and our temperament. And when we need steps and tools which are not available, we need to invent them.

In William's case, this included volunteering to coach his

children's sports teams, running for public office, keeping himself busy and accountable through church and work and school, communicating incessantly on Face Book and through e-mail, and exercising to reduce anxiety and improve his health and fitness, not to mention his self-image. We all know that PTSD is not something from which one ever recovers, but there may well be longer and longer remissions and more and more awareness of how to minimize and neutralize the PTSD symptoms when they do reoccur.

My Story

William's story is one with much to teach us. Consistently throughout his life he has tried to use his greatest challenges, like not being able to shut his mind off, to accomplish something instead of letting himself be defeated. While he has kept himself overscheduled and overbooked, it has worked well for his abundant adrenalin supply that he is almost always not quite where he needs to be with almost always one more thing to accomplish than he could possibly fit in.

William has also chosen activities with his children which work to re-instill in him some of the innocence and play and safety and pleasure which war eroded. He plays sports with his kids and those in the neighborhood during the appropriate seasons and plays video games and Wii and other things off-season. Spending much non-working time with children is a balm to the weary spirit, seeing the fairness of the rules of sports and the joy of personal accomplishment and the mania of a team victory where they have come together and each done his or her part to create success for everyone. The losses, too, are healing, since they are not life and death losses and there is always next year on the baseball diamond.

Getting divorced was another obstacle William chose to see as a new challenge. Contrast Roger's reaction in his case study where he describes his divorce: "I was RAPED, gagged, bound and flung head first into the concrete." William, on the other hand, quickly saw that this was an opportunity for him to get out of a critical, unloving marriage. Being as responsible as he is, this is a step he never could have initiated. After a little thought, he was glad his wife had a boyfriend. He acted quickly. He pushed through a quick dissolution and got the house, the kids and some child support.

Like many other PTSD survivors, William has that illusive character trait, resiliency. Why he has it would make for interesting genetic research. William has an extremely high IQ. Clearly, it doesn't hurt to be bright. While William had the bi-racial and adopted legacies, he did have quite a bit of childhood family support, including extended family and activities like family vacations and reunions and lots of time spent with grandparents. This inter-generational sense of belonging gave William a template for working out his own personal sense of self. The general childhood sanity he experienced also helped him a great deal in getting through and recovering from his Iraq war experiences.

Those veterans of wars after Viet Nam can thank the Viet Nam vets for taking the brunt of America's confusion as we, the country, tried to separate out the dislike of war from the disrespect shown to those who served in the war. Had the Support Our Troops banners and bumper stickers materialized during the Viet Nam war, we could certainly have helped veterans heal somewhat more quickly by not turning on them when they finally straggled home. Insult to injury was never more pronounced than by the treatment Viet Nam vets received from those for whom they fought. Iraq war veterans, like William, at least did not have that with which to contend.

William is doing well as I write this. Life is crazy-busy for him, as always, but he is seeing it differently and working hard to treat himself in newer, saner ways. His exercise, his sober living, his challenge of school, his responsibility for his children and their futures all have been embraced by him as he sees and knows he is a PTSD survivor from before the war, a PTSD survivor because of the war, but a survivor in both cases and a man determined to live his future in freedom--from PTSD as well as other things.

Joy

Her Story

"Oh, Holy Shit! The sky could fall.

I could hyperventilate at the mall. My head

It spins with do's and don'ts. Around the corner

Could be a float from Macy's parade. Why is it here?

Was I supposed to put a tissue there? On no, not me.

I dodged that one. Now I've fallen into Kingdom Come!

Will I get out? Will I get in? Just keep watching!

Or is that a sin?"

This was the first journal entry that Joy gave me. As you can read, there's not a lot of joy in it. But there is a lot of fear. That her name is Joy, made it really ironic when her dad bellowed for her, which he did frequently. "Joy, get down here. What's this puddle on the kitchen counter? Come clean this up!"

"It can come from left, right, above, below.

Best friends, neighbors, siblings, mom.

Any adult, any teacher, even a nice one.

Especially a nice one.

'Why do you keep doing wrong things, Joy?'

Why do people only notice when I screw up?"

Joy was the fifth of nine children. Four were beautiful and brilliant before her, and four were handsome and athletic after her. She was the dreamer. The shrinking violet. In a family of screamers, she was by nature a whisperer. In a family of opinionated, outspoken, loud individualists, she never stood a chance. She simply couldn't get it all.

"Just always be prepared.

And scared. And watchful.

Try to see it coming.

Learn the rules: close door; lights off; energy crisis.

Remember all the stuff he/she/they've told you.

Anyone can be a land mine at any time.

Be super nice, kind, friendly, upbeat, supportive.

Agree when you don't.

Use mind-reading skills.

Assume he/she/they are upset with YOU. What did you DO?"

Joy learned to be scared all the time. As a little girl she learned to feel safe only when grandma was there. But at Christmas time, when she was five, Joy was taken to visit grandma in the hospital.

"They told me she was very sick. I stood at the end of her bed.

She had on a soft blue nightie, was smiling and looked beautiful.

I was enchanted. We looked at each other and we seemed to smile and she seemed to just glow for a long time."

But, Joy was told, grandma's sister went to visit her and while her sister was there, the sister looked out the window, and when she looked back, "Grandma was gone." Joy was already determined to be as attentive as possible. Now, to learn that when you looked out the window people you loved could disappear . . . ?

In third grade the family moved and Joy started at a different Catholic school. She remembers the first time a nun talked to her. "What's 9 from 15?" sister wanted to know. Joy couldn't do it. She hadn't learned negative numbers. Again, "What's 9 from 15?" Joy asked if she meant 15 minus 9? The nun pursed her lips and demanded, "What's 9 from 15?"

The teasing started in fifth grade. "Your hair is out of style! What's wrong with your mom's leg? Don't you have any blue jeans? Only dresses? Saddle shoes? Nobody wears saddle shoes anymore." Joy remembers being teased, tripped, punched, pushed and called "an ugly dog." In gym they had to pick partners and Joy and one other girl were always the last two, left to be together. She'd stand by the nuns at recess to try to stay safe, but the kids realized they could keep up their taunts. The nuns were busy talking to one another. Joy learned she was unprotected.

By sixth grade Joy says the depression started. Actually, she was considering suicide. She took the cap off the nail polish remover and was ready to drink it when something stopped her. She wrote the teacher a note to tell her about it, and the teacher read the note out loud to the class, calling it a story. She also remembers blurting out to her mother how awful she felt and what she was thinking of doing. She recalls her mother had a basket of laundry in her hands when Joy got up the nerve to confess. Her mother frowned at her and kept on walking.

When she was seventeen, her father died. "Our world wasn't just flipped upside down. We weren't even in a world anymore." Joy became the chauffeur to get the younger four to their activities. Mom, who never drove, had to be carted to the store, church, the attorney's office, Social Security and anything else that was necessary.

When someone else was old enough to drive, Joy was released to go to college. In her first semester she walked into a counselor's office and said straight out, "I need some help." She's been in counseling ever since. She's been under the care of a psychiatrist ever since. She's been diagnosed as depressed, bi-polar and having a borderline personality disorder or maybe even an hysterical personality disorder.

She received an education degree and taught middle school for a number of years until one of the large, frightening boys beat her up. Since then she's been unemployed and ill. She's been diagnosed with fibromyalgia, irritable bowel syndrome, rheumatoid arthritis and acid reflux.

Joy is nocturnal. She stays up at least until dawn and sleeps all day, at least until three or four. She never relaxes, never calms down, never takes a full, true, deep breathe. She forgets to eat. She often doesn't get dressed. She's late everywhere she goes. She has had few successes in her life and fewer joys.

"Come, Heavenly King, Creator, Blessed.

Oh, no. It's Not. But now look. Someone's just been shot.

How could I let that horror reign? Just think of those I put in pain.

Time it has passed. I'll go to sleep. But I'll sleep fast.

You never know just what lurks around a sunny corner or with

A child's birth. Good is bad and bad is bad. Stay alert.

Just remember about dad. Don't even blink, you'll miss

a move.

And then a bad thing will explode."

Her Signs

Anxiety and hyper-vigilance have been taken to a new level in Joy's case. Because she was boomed at, hollered at, yelled at, she started very early trying to protect herself from attack. What confounded her was that the other eight siblings didn't seem to mind dad's loud criticism and correction. Nor did they seem to feel deprived by mom's indifference. Only Joy shook and trembled when dad roared and only she begged and pleaded when it was time for mom to go anywhere. Joy did not feel safe. Not with her dad and not with her mom. Not at home and not at school. She simply couldn't remember everything she needed to remember to keep herself safe. And the older she got, the more things there were to remember and the more likely it was she would forget something and so she worried constantly about where "it" would come from--the attack.

Everyone in the house agreed Joy was different. She became the scapegoat. She was easy to blame and she always took the blame. No matter how agreeable and conciliatory she became, she never seemed to be able to cover all the bases. If she tried to take credit for something she had done, she was told to stop bragging. If she tried to take the blame for something she had done, she was told they had expected nothing else from her. The pattern had begun so early that she had no recollection of ever being anything except the bad one.

Joy's nervousness showed in everything she did. She trembled, she shook, she talked too fast, she talked too loud and she never stayed on topic or on task. Virginia Satir has a descriptive term for the Joys of the world: the distracters. You can never get a straight answer from them, because a straight answer has the power to put them in a box. So, instead, distracters dither and sound dumb and wishy-washy and "crazy." "Is it raining?" some one might ask. The distracter would talk for thirty minutes and never tell you whether it was raining, but you'd end up knowing that Mrs. Schmidt had a green scarf and a fat dog. But you had no idea who Mrs. Schmidt was. Nor did you care.

Also, Joy constantly shot herself in the foot. When someone warmed up to her, she tested them and pushed them away. No one was supposed to like her. When she found some medicine that seemed to help, she'd forget to take it. When someone turned out to be a trusted friend or therapist, she'd start missing dates and appointments and stop returning phone calls.

Joy, in addition to being a distracter, became a clown. In a therapy session she would chatter non-stop to keep from having to talk about anything painful. In her friendships and family relationships, she would do a stand-up comic routine that left everyone laughing and no one having any idea what was really going on with Joy. She seemed fine. She sure was funny. And she learned that the best defense was a good, funny offense. But, of course, the offense couldn't be offensive. To prevent that, Joy was always the butt of her own jokes.

Joy has a number of physical and mental health diagnoses. These symptoms of something "wrong" with Joy certainly add to her self-belief that she is different, odd, unusual, maybe even "crazy." The inability of any internist or psychiatrist in finding out what is the matter with her has compounded her neuroses and psychoses. Even the doctors can't determine what's wrong. "Just how messed up am I?" she wonders.

Her Steps

I asked Joy to do something I frequently ask a client to do, which is to go on line and take the Myers/Briggs Personality Inventory. To do this, simply type Myers/Briggs in the search box and about the seventh option down is a test sponsored by Humanetrics. It's free. Seventy-two questions. It gives a printout which contains four letters with a number referencing each letter.

What this test does is divide people into sixteen personality types. These are incredibly helpful for individual therapy and invaluable for marital therapy. The letters and numbers, which correspond to the strength of each variable, tell us what type personality we have.

All of us come wired. We are what we are, and it's all good. No personality type is either bad or unnecessary in the world. The descriptions of personalities and temperaments are vital for self-awareness.

The Myers/Briggs is the most used and best researched test in psychology. An estimated two million people take the Myers/Briggs each year. If you look for books about the Myers/Briggs, you'll find 1, 850, 000 options. The book from which I have learned what little I know about this mammoth topic is David Keirsey's Please Understand Me What I go on to explain about each temperament and personality type is informal information I've gathered over twenty some years as a therapist.

> **Go on-line and type Myers/Briggs in the search box.**
>
> **The test provided by Humanetrics is free and reliable.**
>
> **You'll be given a one page printout with your personality type.**

After you take the test you will find yourself with four letters. If your second letter is an "S," you will find either a "J" or a "P" for your fourth letter. This means your temperament is that of an SJ, a sensing judge, or an SP, a sensing perceiver. If your second letter is an "N," you will find either a "T" or an "F" for your third letter. That means you are an NF, an intuitive feeler, or an NT, an intuitive thinker. These then are the four temperaments: SJ, SP, NF, or NT. It is these that we're going to talk about because it is the unearthing of Joy's temperament which was so helpful in her therapy.

> **SJs are the responsible worker bees of the world.**
>
> **They keep the societal train well-greased and on the tracks.**

SJs make the world go round. They keep it spinning. They are the rule-followers who do what they should and understand the world through their senses. If they can't see it, hear it, taste it, touch it, smell it and feel it (feel it in a kinesthetic sense, not an emotional sense), then it doesn't exist to them. That's the "S" influence. The "J" influence is that these people are planners, organizers and they like to accomplish things in a coherent, consistent, sequential way.

George Washington and Dwight Eisenhower are two notable SJs. The squirrel who plans for winter by storing away nuts and the beaver who perseveres as he gnaws his way though logs and branches to build his dam home are animals which represent the SJ. Thirty-eight percent of the population are SJs.

Sensing and judging individuals are caring but not usually affectionate. They are sensitive but not normally empathic. Their great strengths are responsibility, loyalty and honest trustworthiness. One of their typical weaknesses is judging and resenting those who are not as devoted or accountable.

> **SPs are the life and energy of the world. They were born to play!**
>
> **They get off the train for adventures and love the detours.**

SPs are the polar opposite of SJs. If they can get someone else to handle the drudgery of daily life, they're all for it. The "S" influence is sensing, like the "S" in the "SJ." So SPs perceive the world through their senses, too. Like the SJ, the SP is also a realist, but typically SPs define reality differently. The SPs usually decide, really, what does it matter if we make the beds and do the dishes? They'll just need to be re-done tomorrow, so why stress over it? Let's eat, drink and be merry.

The "P" of the SP is perceiving. The perceiver, when paired with the sensor, is impetuous, spontaneous and primed for adventure. There is no fore-thought here. Lights. Camera. Action. John F. Kennedy and Ernest Hemmingway were two well-known and representative SPs. Where SJs are the rule-followers, SPs are the rule-breakers. Well, it's just that the rules don't apply to them. If you're not an SP, get out of the fast lane. The fox is the animal used to portray the SP, wily, creative, conniving. SPs are also often artistic and musical and great with their hands. The SP is the name on the wall: "For a good time, call. . . ." Obviously, a slight down-side to this temperament might be a lack of accountability. Paying the bills? Going to work? Responsibility? Oh, don't be such a stick in the mud.

Seventy-five percent of the world is sensing. Half of them are SJs and half are SPs. These folks see the world and everything in it as black or white, right or wrong, good or bad. There is no slack to be had from an SJ or an SP and there are no multiple realities or alternative explanations. It is what it is, they will tell us.

The "Ns" of the world, on the other hand, only a quarter of the population, live in a gray world of abstraction. The "N" temperament is not black and white. Those who are intuitive are subjective thinkers (test questions with multiple choices and plenty of room for philosophizing) rather than sensing, objective thinkers (right/wrong and true/false questions and answers).

> **NTs are the "head" of the world.**
>
> **They are the thinkers, the analyzers, the architects of ideas. NTs think outside the box and move society forward.**
>
> **They design new trains that don't require tracks.**

When intuition is paired with thinking, we get the twelve percent of the population who "think" outside the box. These folks can look at things the way they've always been done and see new ways to do them. They conceptualize things which have never existed and create the new and different. They're known as the "architects of ideas." The owl is the animal which epitomizes the NT with its ability to see so much more than the rest of us see.

NTs are typically emotionally cool and aloof. They are often arrogant, or at least seen as arrogant because the niceties of social interaction are meaningless to them. Notable NT's are Einstein and Descartes. Society would sit still and vegetate were it not for the imaginative, intuitive thinkers who are responsible for most of the progress of the human race.

> **NFs are the "heart" of the world. It would be a cold, cruel world, indeed, were it not for their empathy and warmth.**
>
> **They bring faith, hope and charity along on the train.**

And now we come to the last twelve percent of the population, the NFs. (If you've just added up the percentages to make sure they equal 100, you're either an SJ who is also a T or an NT who is also a J. If it never occurred to you to add up the numbers you either don't care, SPs of the world, or you wouldn't want to hurt my feelings by adding them up in case I'm wrong, NFs.)

This is where the Myers/Briggs put Joy and this information was vital to understanding how she was traumatized by a childhood everyone else in the family seemed to simply accept and endure. Joy is an INFP. Only about one of every one hundred people has this personality type.

We'll talk about the NF first, to finish our discussion of the four temperaments. Then we'll talk about Joy's personality and how it might have played a part in her woundedness.

The twelve percent of the world who are NFs are the "heart" of the world. They feel outside the box, in contrast to the NTs who think outside the box. Mahatma Gandhi and Eleanor Roosevelt are well-known NFs, and if any president in recent history would be an NF, it would be someone like Jimmy Carter, creator of Habitat for Humanity and winner of the Nobel Peace Prize. (NFs are very, very big on peace). History buffs would tell us he wasn't a very effective president. He wouldn't be. NFs tend to be empathic idealists. They see the potential in people, not people as they actually are. NFs are dreamers, not realists. A job like President of the United States of America demands realism, savvy and the ability to make snap, hard life and death decisions. Don't send an NF.

NFs are the sensitive children. They are the kids who stay in from recess to play with the kid in the cast. They worry themselves sick when the teacher doesn't come to school. They are friends with their grandparents. They want the admiration and affection of all and they give it back ten-fold.

The dolphin is the animal that represents these soft, make-no-waves dreamers. NFs preach and counsel faith, hope and charity. They believe that everyone is worthwhile. They explain that criminals had bad childhoods. They argue that we need to be green and save the planet for our children. NFs are the hippies who want to make love, not war, and if you have an NF as a friend, you always have someone on your side. They'll drop what they're doing and rush to your aid, not out of responsibility like the SJ, but out of love. To the cynic and the realist, NFs are the patsies, the naïve bleeding hearts.

Joy was, of course, one of these tender children, the ones frequently described as "too sensitive." If these children are protected and sheltered from the harsh and the heartless at too young an age, they grow up to be like orchids: indomitable bloomers. But they've got to have the early soft and gentle coddling.

SJs need to be taught how to play and be carefree. SPs need to be taught how to be responsible and accountable. NTs typically need some lessons in compassion and social intercourse. If SJs and NTs don't learn their lessons early, they seem to self-correct when their hormones scream out for connection. SPs learn their lessons from society and the need for a steady paycheck. But NF children probably demand the most compassionate and understanding parents. They have got to be protected while they grow strong. When this happens, they are passionate adults, fighting for causes and people and they are resilient members of society.

Joy is an example of how a vulnerable, budding NF can be traumatized by life. Her dad was a critical, controlling screamer, her mom overwhelmed and unresponsive. The siblings tramped her down, the nuns broke her spirit and the thoughtless, cruel children broke her heart. She learned that people died if you took your eyes off them, even if only to look out the window, and she learned that she was not safe anywhere, anytime, with anyone.

Her Steps

In addition to the Myers/Briggs, to which we refer often, Joy has done a multitude of different things. In therapy she has done artwork, poetry writing and voluminous journaling. All these right-brained activities seem to unearth trauma in ways that our conscious brains won't permit. The unconscious right-brained information sneaks through under the radar.

Joy has tried numerous medications for her mental and physical health issues. Nothing seems to make as much difference as she needs it to make. Medication for Joy's issues has been difficult to determine, and perhaps the various combinations have simply not been put together in the right order yet.

My suggestion to Joy that the root of her issues is that she is a posttraumatic stress survivor has probably done more to help Joy than anything else. This diagnosis was a relief to her. There is no stigma to having been traumatized. You didn't do it to yourself. Admittedly, we have to work on this point constantly with survivors of abuse, but gradually it does become clear. They reacted to what was done to them in the only ways they knew how. Blaming themselves keeps them in perpetual victimization and traps their abusers inside their own psyches.

Blaming myself for my own trauma and abuse keeps me in perpetual victimization and traps the abuser inside my own psyche.

Joy and I have frequently made schedules. Her nocturnal hours continually throw her out of rhythm. She simply can't get to sleep most nights, her fear of the night and the dark unknown is too strong. She remembers as a little girl crawling soundlessly into the bed two of her sisters shared and only there, with them, being able to sleep. We haven't gotten to the reason for this and perhaps never will. I am hopeful we'll get the little orchid strong enough that she can close her eyes in the dark.

Joy also forgets to eat except for junk food, sugar and caffeine especially. She has come to therapy in pajamas and in various states of being uncombed, unmade-up, and inadequately dressed. Please understand this woman is clean and pretty and delightful. She simply doesn't know how to care for herself or how to nurture herself. I frequently ask clients to find a childhood picture and place it on their dresser so they look at it often. Then I ask them to care for themselves as they would care for that little child. Joy has done this. The results are disappointing. She has a terrible time being good to herself, even the most basic aspects of good, like eating and sleeping and getting dressed for the weather.

Joy has gotten a lot of meaning from reading <u>War and the Soul</u>. For Joy and another client I'm seeing right now who has a similar story, Ed Tick's book has been a breakthrough. Although written for veterans of military wars, it is easy to see how domestic war veterans can be similarly shell-shocked and traumatized. We send men and women to military service at eighteen--clearly, much too young. But wars in the homes of innocent children start much earlier than that.

The other similar client, we'll call her Nancy, was molested by her brother. When she told, she was not believed and was punished for making up such things. Her brother died in a car accident and his pictures are spread throughout the family home like objects on a shrine. She cannot go home without throwing up. One of her sisters cannot go home at all. All these years later, when there is no doubt whatsoever about what this brother did, since it affected four sisters, neither parent has yet been able to say the simple words, "I'm sorry." He is a hero and no one had better contest that fact.

While Nancy's childhood abuse memories are specific, Joy's are vague. For example, she remembers that her grandfather got drunk a lot and she was told to stay up with him while he drank and was assigned to get him up the steps and into his bed. She also remembers one of the neighbors from her early childhood as always giving her the creeps. She recalls holding her little arms out straight to ward him off. Her memory stops there. We know no more right now. We may never have additional information. That's okay. We don't need facts. This isn't a seeking of justice. This is a giving of mercy and Joy is beginning to understand that this mercy needs to come from herself to herself. Here's one of the most recent things she wrote:

Here's My Shot in the Foot

Giving all up with every fiber of my being.

    Too fast,

    Too easily,

    Too freely.

Trusting completely

    Without reserve

    Or reflection

    Disregarding my tiny voice.

Not protecting parts of me

    I know are too vulnerable and valuable

    To fling about like old bird seed.

    Over and around

    An unsuspecting and unaware
    World.

Just throwing my flood gates open

    And wondering why a friend

    Didn't just flow with the current.

    Figured she could swim.

    Doesn't everyone? No.

    Won't she grab the big round tube

    If I have perfect aim? No. No.

I forgot to save my heart again.

I am repeating a toxic pattern in a new way:

    "Just too kind for you to hurt me"

    "Just too nice for you not to love me"

"Just too humorous for you to lose interest in me"

"Just too agreeable to be irritating to you"

And the air is sucked out of my lungs

Even as I remember people

I let go under that current and damn them anyway.

Who needs him?

Who needs her?

Not me.

I forgot to save myself -

As myself,

As a child of God,

As a good person,

As a worthy person

A writer,

A comic,

A friend.

Lifted 10 fifty-pound bags

By myself today.

It's better with a friend,

But not impossible to do by myself.

I see I was strong enough,

Even if a few muscles were pulled

Stretched

Tender.

I'm still here.

There's prayer and tomorrow

And right now.

I still have me

Spirit whispers.

Then, I turn the page and write.

My Story

It is impossible not to love Joy. She is kind, charming, complimentary and frustrating as hell. That tendency she has to distract and go off track could be very annoying, if I didn't understand why she does it. Joy needs to protect herself. She is one of those clients to whom I will inevitably say, as I lie on my death bed, "NOW, do you trust me?" And, of course, I do understand that it is not about me. But it breaks my easily trusting heart when children have been treated in ways which prohibit them from ever trusting again.

Joy has been wounded and hurting since she was a toddler. She is unemployed and struggling through life. It is my determined commitment to keep working with all the nurturing and gentleness she didn't receive as a child and to help her find herself and build a strong, resilient stem on this orchid so she can bloom and flourish and give the world her wonderful, abundant gifts of love and humor. And if you are a stray dog or cat, I suggest you head to Joy's house. She cannot resist your innocent little eyes.

Carrie

Her Story

Carrie looked like the all-American girl. That was my first thought when I saw her in the waiting room. But she seemed frozen to the chair. I took her hand and led her to my office. She sat like a robot. Neither of us spoke. She was a deer in the headlights.

"Start wherever you want to, Carrie. Tell me whatever comes to mind." "I decided to take a vacation with a friend, a guy, Mark. We kinda met and dated a year and a half ago. He'd randomly text me and just say, 'Hello.'

I had just ended a long-term relationship with Patrick. I so badly wanted to book a vacation to go to Atlanta and see my best girlhood friend,

Amanda. She and this other friend of ours, Jess, lived and worked there.

Mark said he'd go with me.

We arrived on a Saturday afternoon and all had lunch together. We had a great time. Mark and I went back to our hotel room and showered and got ready for dinner.

We went to this cool new country and western place. My friends and their boyfriends and two other couples and Mark and me. We met a couple friends of one of the guys. One was a guy named Pete. Within the first two seconds this kid creeped me out, but I was friendly and made small talk. I can remember him trying to ask me to impress me if he should get a Ferrari or a Lamborghini. I asked him what he did for a living.

He told me he worked for a phone company.

We walked to two other bars. Amanda and Jess and I laughed together and danced together all night. We were all too intoxicated to drive, so we decided to take a cab back to Amanda's apartment complex where she and Jess and their boyfriends all lived.

I remember partly falling asleep in the cab and waking up to fight about who was going to pay for it. At that point I was uncomfortable with dealing with Mark and his 'allegations' about going back to the hotel room together. So Amanda took me to her apartment where I fell asleep on her couch.

Mark threw a fit like a baby and wanted me to feel bad that he was taking a cab back to our hotel room. Thinking he was throwing a good temper tantrum, he took a cab and left me there.

Amanda came back to check on me and put clean sheets on her bed and had her boyfriend pick me up and carry me to her room. They left and went to his apartment across the hall.

Next thing I knew, I half woke up and someone was taking my clothes off. I couldn't move. I couldn't open my eyes. I knew I had to do something, but I couldn't. It was like my body was in shock. I drifted out, and when I came back, it was because I felt someone inside me.

I told him to get the fuck off me. How dare he take advantage of me? I remember sobbing and thinking I had to do something, but where was I? Where were my clothes? Where was my purse with my phone? Who would I call? I was too embarrassed and too drunk. Who would believe me? I had to wait.

A couple of hours later I woke up, immediately crying. I started to panic.

I started to remember what happened. But what did happen? Was I hurt? Did I hurt? Where were my clothes with my purse and my cell phone?

Who actually did this to me?

There was a door closed which was Jess's bedroom. I had to suck up my embarrassment and ask them for clothes and for help.

I knocked softly on the door. I waited for an answer as I stood there with a down comforter wrapped around me and tears streaming down my face.

To my astonishment, Pete answered the door. He asked me if I was crying and I ignored him, asking him what the fuck happened last night. He stared with a blank face at me. I spotted my clothes and purse, dressed in two seconds and ran across the hall, calling Amanda.

I don't remember what I said to her. I know I said in a

panicky voice, 'I'm not sure what happened.'

I have a flashback of two things. One, waking up to find someone taking off my clothes and thinking I had nothing to worry about. Someone was taking off my clothes but there was no way anything would happen. I was not in control of my body and no one would take advantage of that. Two, feeling someone inside me. This was very uncomfortable and I knew I needed someone to stop. How could they do this to me? It felt like I couldn't move. I couldn't believe that someone would believe that I wanted this. But it hurt. And I couldn't move. I finally got the strength to say, 'What the fuck. Get off me!'

Telling Amanda that, I couldn't believe this. I think my mind and my body were in shock.

Amanda got her boyfriend and we tried to piece what we could together.

I said Mark went back to the hotel in a cab. I remembered feeling too uncomfortable going back to the hotel with him. I knew I had too many drinks and didn't want to put myself in a bad situation.

Raging, pissed, Amanda walked over to her apartment to Pete and said something like 'What did you do to her?' Pete didn't know. Amanda asked if he had sex with me and he said, 'If she said I did, then I did.'

Amanda told Pete we were going to the hospital and the truth would come out.

Amanda held my hand and we cried the whole way to the hospital.

While we were waiting at the hospital, Amanda called Mark. She told him something bad happened to me and he asked, 'With Pete?' She wanted to know why he'd say that. He said I told him last night that Pete was creepy and then when I fell asleep in the car, Pete was rubbing my leg. Mark told him to stop, but Pete actually did it twice.

We walked back into the exam room and a very sweet nurse started asking me a million questions. She asked me if I wanted to press charges and I wasn't sure. I wanted to think maybe it didn't happen or maybe it didn't go really far for a long period of time. I knew I felt him inside me, I just was hoping the nurse would tell me it was all a bad dream. As she examined me, the awakening news was when she told me, 'Wow. I don't think we've ever collected this much semen.'

I almost threw up. Amanda and I both started bawling. I just kept saying,

'It's real. I can't believe it. I'm a statistic. I can't believe this happened to me. Intimacy is so special for me. Will I be scarred forever?'

The police officers and the volunteers from rape crisis were all very kind and helpful to Carrie. When she and Amanda got back to the apartment complex, her friends were standing outside waiting for her. The girls got her in the bathtub and the guys got on line to change her flight home. Amanda's boyfriend took her aside and talked to her. He was helpful, Carrie says, with tips about a therapist. He also told her she wasn't responsible for any of this. He said no guy, friend or boyfriend, has the right to expect anything from a girl. All her friends told the detective that Carrie was not the kind of girl to have sex with a guy without a long-standing, deep relationship. When Carrie got off the plane at home, her father was waiting for her with flowers, a card and tears in his eyes. Carrie said the only time she'd ever seen him cry was at his mother's funeral and she didn't remember him ever buying anyone flowers, not even her mother.

Her Signs

Guilt was Carrie's major symptom. She knew she made some mistakes. She said she shouldn't have traveled with someone she didn't know very well, because it was in preventing something happening with him that she set herself up for something happening later and with someone else. She shouldn't have had so much to drink. She shouldn't have put herself in a vulnerable situation.

That's all true, I agreed. But what happened, rape, is a criminal act. No matter what we do, whether we dance down the street naked at three in the morning or sleep on a park bench, we do not deserve to be the victim of a crime. Just because you carry a purse doesn't mean you are complicit in having your purse snatched. Just because you own a house doesn't mean you are agreeable to being broken into and robbed. Just because you're driving alone in a convertible doesn't mean you are asking to be car-jacked. Human behavior, from the most cautious to the most foolhardy, has nothing to do with being at the wrong place at the wrong time with the wrong person. Criminals don't wear badges that say, "Hi, I'm one of the bad guys."

I remember, in fact, seeing a picture of a man who had abducted and murdered a number of little girls. He was wearing a herringbone blazer, white shirt and tie. He was very nice looking. I stared and stared at his picture because I knew, in the wrong place at the wrong time, I would have talked to him. He looked absolutely normal. He just happened to be a sociopath.

People often blame themselves and each other for being victimized as well as for accidents. "Weren't you looking? Were you going too fast? Were you fiddling with the radio?" Now why on earth do you suppose they're called "accidents"? Because they are accidental, not intended or premeditated. No one says, "I think I'll skid into that nice big, red stop sign over there and bash up my car and maybe break my nose." As accidental as accidents are, so, too, is it accidental who becomes a crime victim and who, through nothing but dumb luck, doesn't.

Carrie was afraid. She felt absolutely paranoid about leaving her apartment and walking to her car. She hated leaving her job in the dark. She couldn't go to the mall or to the grocery store alone. And she definitely couldn't sleep. Every sound woke her and then she lay awake shaking and terrified that "something bad" was going to happen. She didn't have bad dreams or flashbacks. She battled the unknown. What else happened? How did he get my jeans off? Why couldn't I move?

The hospital doctor had ordered blood work. He wanted to check for drugs which might have immobilized Carrie. Had someone, Pete or somebody else, put something in one of Carrie's drinks? Adding to Carrie's fear was the inexplicable fact that the hospital lost her blood work. It simply disappeared. Had Pete gotten into the hospital and destroyed it? That seemed ludicrous, but so did the fact that her results vanished.

Carrie withdrew from life other than her family commitments and work. She continued going to church every Sunday, having dinner at her grandparents' house, and shopping with her mom, but she didn't date and didn't drink at all for almost a year. When she did start dating again, she would meet someone somewhere, arriving in her own car and driving herself home.

Carrie pressed charges and that caused her a lot of anxiety and a lot of second guessing. Was it the right thing to do? What if Pete hadn't really meant it or if he was truly sorry and her pressing charges would ruin his life? Maybe he'd lose his job and be labeled a sexual predator? What if the case went to trial and she had to tell her story in front of a jury? They'd all sit there judging her and deciding that she was a bad girl who had "asked for it." Every time a new part of the criminal process came around, Carrie's anxiety rose.

Her Steps

I had been to a Belleruth Naparstek workshop two weeks before Carrie came in my door. The name of the workshop was "Reversing Panic Attacks, Acute Stress and PTSD." As they say in comedy, timing is everything.

Belleruth Naparstek believes that guided imagery is a powerful tool in healing PTSD. She suggests from her massive research that trauma is stored in the body as an undiluted mass. Trauma is not something that happens to us cognitively, and therefore talk therapy, cognitive therapy, is not completely effective. (I have not found this to be so, but I will admit it is a slow process.)

Symbol and metaphor, she recommends, are a safer, kinder more efficient method for working with PTSD survivors. We need to use immersive right-brained techniques, not the logical, rational tools of the left brain. Imagery takes us to an altered state beyond clock time and gives us a multi-sensory approach which is body based. We have long known that PTSD symptoms are stored in the senses as the smell of his after shave, the sound of a fire truck that went by in the midst of the trauma, the feel of something scratchy like whiskers, just to name some examples. If trauma is stored in the senses, then trauma will be dislodged through the senses, too.

Naparstek is a Jungian. It was Carl Jung who said that we humans process information in terms of archetypal themes and figures. Jung proposed that story, fairy tale and prayer constitute the ground for healing. Clarissa Pinkola Estes wrote her beautiful Women Who Run With the Wolves based on these same ideas. She and Naparstek agree with the Jungian concept that we need a non-ordinary, sacred space, some magical or mystical or divine energy, and a ritual of transformation so we can shed the old trauma memories stuffed inside us, and create and integrate anew.

As we've said before, there is scientific, neurophysiological and biophysical research and data explaining what happens in the brain and in the body. I encourage you to read about this and learn about it if it interests you. For many of us, it is sufficient to know that things actually change in our brains and bodies when we're traumatized. We have to reverse those physical and biological rushes and create new pathways to understanding life and our ability to deal with it.

Fascinating new studies are finding that some medications, beta-blockers for one, when given to a trauma victim in the emergency room, can halt the brain from storing trauma as trauma. We can medically interrupt the trauma response. These developments will be fascinating to watch.

Because I was newly acquainted with Belleruth Naparstek's ideas and Carrie seemed such a likely candidate, I asked her if she would be willing to try some guided imagery. I explained my understanding of why it might be helpful for her. Guided imagery, then, became the first step Carrie and I took in helping her heal from her trauma.

At each appointment she talked about where she was in her process, what she was feeling, what she was fearing, what she had tried in terms of self-care and self-talk. In the last fifteen minutes or so, I put on some relaxation music and I read to her from Belleruth Naparstek's texts of guided imagery exercises. Carrie was, indeed, transported to another plane, definitely out of clock time and real space and she reported she found an unprecedented place for relaxation and safety. (Invisible Heroes is the Naparstek book that I use. There are also tapes of her exercises, but she recommends that the individual therapist's voice might be more effective for some clients.)

Carrie, as you have read, also immediately began a journal. "I'm writing and starting a journal because my therapist that I met with yesterday said it would be helpful for me" was her first entry. I did and I do. I suggested to Carrie that she write down everything that happened in as much detail as she could remember, not judging what she was writing or editing it, but simply writing it out of her body and onto paper. That way, weeks or months later, she wouldn't have to try to recollect the bits and pieces, nor would she need to store them in her memory. "Write it down and don't look at it unless you need it for something" was what I suggested to her. It was Carrie's word for word journal entries which became the basis of her story here. Indeed, after she wrote the trauma down, she never looked at it again. She handed me her journal without ever needing to revisit the sequence of events.

Carrie did a number of things to feel safer in her apartment. She got a roommate. A male. A friend of a friend who was well-known to her family and who had a girlfriend. This was strictly a business acquaintance. Because she wasn't allowed to have a dog, she got a cat. Feeling the attack cat might be a bit ineffectual, she also had a security system installed. This really helped her sleep, since it guaranteed that she would not be surprised in the middle of the night. In addition, her dad put a good, heavy lock on her bedroom door. Don't even ask if all these things aren't just crutches. When you break a leg, there's a reason why you use crutches for a while. So it is in other cases, as well.

Carrie became much more cognizant of her surroundings and now walks out of work or a store only in the daylight or with someone else. She was given a pepper spray keychain by a friend, and she holds it and her car keys in her hands at all times. She is prepared to hit the panic button on her keychain or spray anyone who surprises her. Carrie will ask questions later. Where previously embarrassment was a deterrent to good security practices, she is now willing to risk embarrassment if it means keeping herself safe.

Carrie is determined to use her experience to help others. It is with her permission and encouragement that I have used her journal verbatim. She is hoping to give speeches to young girls about their own safety and crime prevention. This bright, resilient, young woman is doing what it takes to transition from victim to survivor. She is going to make this trauma count for something by doing everything in her power to save others from her own nightmare.

My Story

Would that all trauma stories had an ending like this. But, then, not many had a beginning like this. Carrie was predisposed to recover from her trauma. She had no early childhood trauma. She came from a strong, loving, intergenerational family. She had a firm and helpful (read: non-guilt inducing) faith background and she had a great deal of healthy self-esteem. This college graduate was working two jobs, dressed to the nines, had a ton of friends and felt good about herself physically, mentally and socially.

When the trauma occurred, Carrie had supportive friends who rallied around her. The hospital personnel, the police officers, and the rape crisis staff all treated her with dignity and lack of judgment. She was never blamed for being a victim. Finally, this trauma was out of the realm of her entire life's experiences. The later the trauma and the stronger the psychic house one has built when the trauma happens, the greater the likelihood of full and complete recovery.

At this writing, Carrie has a new boyfriend. They dated for

a while and slid easily into love. They spent the night together and had sex before she had gotten up the nerve to tell him about her trauma. She cried afterward, silently, trying not to let him know, and in the middle of the night, she woke him to tell him she had to go home. He was puzzled, but walked her to the car and kissed her goodnight and told her how enchanted he was. They spent the next night together, and this time there was no trauma and no need to escape. They've been together ever since.

She told him about the rape and the fact that someone named Pete had been sent to prison for what he had done to her. Her boyfriend, of course, immediately offered to do Pete bodily harm. Testosterone is so predictable. She described Pete and asked her boyfriend to never question her if she says she has to leave a restaurant or a bar or a play or a baseball game because Pete, or more likely, someone with similar physical characteristics appears. Of course, he would honor her need to be safe and he would protect her in every way possible. For the second time since the trauma, she saw a guy who doesn't usually cry, cry with her and for her.

She is feeling stable and strong. She is happy and healthy. I wish all case studies ended this way. But, again I stress, they are much more likely to end this way if they begin this way.

Carrie says she will always stay in therapy. She loves the safe place to say anything and be accepted. She never realized how important it was to have an objective ear and heart to listen to her fears and woes and dreams and silliness. She is looking for and applying for a job which is more suited to her strengths. If asked seriously, I believe Carrie would say she does not regret her trauma because it taught her so much and helped her to believe in herself and her resiliency. I know this new knowledge and the additional coping skills she acquired will always be an asset to her. She was an amazing girl when she came into therapy, and she is an amazing woman now. Trauma demands that we grow up and grow into who we have become. Carrie did. It will serve her well all her life.

One additional comment about Carrie as an example of a survivor of rape or incest or any kind of sexual abuse. The body has what is called "tissue memory." This means that the body itself stores sensations of pain and pleasure. The body can't tell the difference between the touch of a rapist and the touch of a devoted lover. The body simply knows what feels good and what feels bad. This is an essential issue to any man or woman who is with any woman or man who has been sexually abused.

I will frequently ask a significant other to come in and let me talk to him or her about some precautions that could be taken to keep flashbacks from occurring. These precautions center around making sure your lover knows it's you. Talk to him or her. Do not surprise him or her. No sudden moves, no coming up from behind, and no jumping out. The survivor of abuse must have a chance to know who is doing the touching. Use soft lights and keeping engaged through conversation and eye contact. These things reassure the survivor that he or she is safe now. This is absolutely essential.

Carrie and I spent a great deal of time talking about what it might be like to have sex again. We talked about tissue memory and the possibilities of flashbacks, and I suggested to her that she keep her mind engaged, keep present, and keep her eyes open.

I also talked to her about something which plagues many survivors of sexual assault:

Sometimes there are aspects of the sexual contact which were pleasant. The guilt of this is often overwhelming. "How could I have possibly enjoyed any part of that? What's wrong with me?" Nothing is wrong with you. Your body can't tell the difference. Your body acted in the only way it knows how--physically. Your body didn't make an emotional or a moral decision to enjoy some portion of a brutal, despicable event. Your body reacted physically. These two areas of awareness, precautions for significant others and the possibility of remembering some pleasure from something awful, are incredibly helpful for survivors since they may prevent problems which could grow and fester if left unacknowledged.

■

Susan

Her Story

This last case study will appear under one name although it is a compilation of a great many different stories. What these stories have in common is a diagnosis: compassion fatigue or secondary posttraumatic stress. This is the PTSD of the witness, the by-stander, the observer. This is the trauma which comes from repeated proximity to trauma. Trauma is traumatizing, and being the witness and listener to repeated and frequent traumas is traumatizing, as well.

There are millions of us who, with moderately strong psychic houses, are determined to undertake lives of service. In fact, we entered the adult world with a mission to help. We are the police officers, firefighters, doctors, nurses, medics, social workers, ministers, priests, rabbis, therapists, teachers, corrections officers, wardens and the inner city workers.

We don't all suffer from secondary PTSD, but some of us do. What is different about us? Clearly, there are a few main distinctions. First, our temperament predisposes us to absorb trauma. As we talked about in Joy's story, NFs on the Myers/Briggs test are the great absorbers. We are the thin-skinned folk who cry at the AT&T ads and actually feel each other's pain, which is the meaning of empathy. This is our great strength and our great weakness. I would estimate about two-thirds to three-quarters of all therapists are NFs.

A second susceptibility to PTSD comes from having had trauma elsewhere in our lives. Trauma builds on trauma. Early trauma, especially childhood trauma, seems to make us more likely to absorb later incidents as trauma. A medical analogy is that you had to have had the chicken pox to be susceptible to shingles. Seems unfair, but, as many of us are fond of saying, it is what it is.

A third predisposing factor is the nature of the trauma or the degree to which we are exposed. I'm reminded of a colleague telling me about something she witnessed in the emergency room. It should have been an uncomplicated birth. Instead, everything went wrong. She described it in gruesome detail, which is how she remembered it, and the way it was imprinted on her brain and in her heart. I'll spare you the images and simply say that this jarring tragedy will always haunt her and will remain cemented inside her memory banks. So, the horror of the trauma is certainly a factor.

One's mental state at the time of the trauma and immediately thereafter is a fourth factor to be considered. Someone who works every day with low level trauma, for example, doing police work, or staffing the emergency department, is more prepared for horror than, say, Jackie Kennedy who was enjoying a calm ride in a convertible, surrounded by Secret Service men, the sun shining brightly on her pink suit when unfathomable trauma came from out of nowhere to alter her life.

What happens immediately following the trauma is also an important component. I worked with a police officer who was repeatedly shot at when he arrived on a domestic violence call. The shooter then turned the gun on his wife and held her hostage. The SWAT team was called and arrived with a crisis intervention specialist whose job it was to de-brief and de-traumatize the officer. Being in a situation where one is tended to and treated with respect is a great asset. Think again of Carrie's story and her friends who surrounded her and "carried" her.

And then there is the Chinese water torture type of trauma which affects many therapists. It's the combined weight of the water that does you in, as well as the constant dripping. A few drops alone would not take you under, but add enough drips and we've got secondary PTSD.

Let me give you an example of what a therapist might hear in one day.

Hour one: a young college student has lost a parent and a favorite grandparent weeks apart and is in despair.

Hour two: A thirty-something woman is a sexual abuse survivor. This week alone she had her car repossessed and the relative with whom she was living has asked her to relocate somewhere else. In other words, she's been kicked out of her home and has no transportation.

Hour three: A woman in her fifties has been married for thirty years to a wealthy, successful businessman who happens to be addicted to cocaine and has decided to take shooting lessons and join the NRA.

Hour four: A woman, this one in her late forties, a cancer survivor, has never worked because her husband wanted her to stay home and raise the children. After almost thirty years of marriage he has decided to move out, stop paying the bills, send the house into foreclosure and declare bankruptcy.

Hour five: A high school student's parents are divorcing.

Dad has actually moved in with a new girlfriend and her children although there is no divorce yet, leaving mom with a house she can't afford, no car, and their four kids. The client, at fifteen, is the oldest.

Hour six: A forty-something man explained that his wife has had an affair with a co-worker and, consequently, lost her job. The co-worker, her boss, retained his job. The man loves his wife, but how do you get past three years of lies and a secret life?

Hour seven: Two former high school sweethearts reconnected after a dozen years and quickly married. Almost immediately he got laid off and, while staying home, expanded his interest in pornography to an eight hour a day addiction.

Hour eight: One member of a blended family arrives to start therapy. The family includes a mother-in-law with dementia and a high school aged son with a pregnant girlfriend. The new client reports feeling anxious.

If a friend had one of these stories to tell, you'd go home with a headache. But on they come, one after another, and through it all you feel like the emergency room doctor watching the woman who overdosed on Tylenol and knowing there is nothing you can do, or the police officer at the scene of the wreck where, while waiting for the Jaws of Life, the hand in his grip goes limp, or the firefighter who has to bring out of the house the small, lifeless body he found in the crib.

There is a helplessness so profound that it can be disabling. How does one stand by and watch the horror of life? How does one clean up after the careless smoker? How does one sit and listen as the stories tell themselves and the tellers empty their pathos into our laps? Well, most therapists do it very well. But, that doesn't mean it doesn't take a toll. The toll is called secondary PTSD.

Our Signs

Anxiety, depression, apathy, cynicism, alcohol, drugs, shopping, eating, gambling, watching television, religious fixations, sick jokes, fast cars, affairs, isolation, agnosticism, computer games, incessant reading, over exercising, and a fascination with vitamins, make-up and anti-aging creams are a few of the symptoms of secondary PTSD. In short, therapists self-medicate in every way others self-medicate. And it doesn't make a bit of difference that we might have some good reasons or some benign intent. The possibility for a therapist to fall into a really bad habit or slip into an addiction is ever present. Life is dangerous for all of us, and for those witnessing pain, life is painfully dangerous, just as it is for those actually experiencing pain.

For those who live in and around pain, Life is painfully dangerous.

Anxiety is one of the most prevalent symptoms of secondary PTSD. Our brain chemistry seems to accustom itself to the little shocks and jolts of the trauma we hear all day. I know I sometimes feel myself bracing for what's coming, preparing, as if I could prepare, and then second-guessing. Should I have said that? Did I miss what the client was trying to tell me? While some therapists, because of their anxiety, get too sure of answers and start making pronouncements instead of offering possibilities, others of us become even more unsure, and our anxiety slows us down as though we are less likely to make mistakes if we move more tentatively.

The anxiety a therapist experiences is understandable. Someone comes in and offers us one side of a story for an hour at a stretch, and we're expected to guide them to do things such as stay married, separate from parents, leave their spouse of decades, change jobs or place an elderly relative in a nursing home. Clients come to see us when they find themselves in the midst of life's turmoil, unsure of which way to turn, and they'd like some objective guidance, often some moral guidance. I'd like a quarter for every time I've asked a client what he or she thought the high road would be in this case and then suggested he or she walk that path. Are we trained for this? Yes, as much as one can be trained. You can train a teacher or a doctor or a therapist, but most of us are born for our roles and the training simply makes conscious much that we know intuitively. None of that, however, negates the anxiety.

I can feel when my anxiety is the worst. It will wake me in the night and I'll find myself replaying a conversation I had with someone or rehearsing a conversation I'm soon to have. My anxiety is also bad when I lose my vocabulary or find myself starving right after I've eaten. These are clues to me that I'm not paying attention to myself, not staying in the present. Another indicator to me that I'm feeling anxious is my need to supply answers. In my calmer states, I'm content to listen to and be with a client. In my anxious state, I feel like I need to fix things.

I get disorganized when I start feeling depressed. I'll let my paperwork slide, my handwriting becomes sloppy and my desk starts piling up with stuff I usually handle efficiently. I stay in my office and close my door, eschewing people when I'm sliding into a depression. I'll say "no" when friends want me to do things with them and I'll isolate over weekends, too. Colleagues tell me they find themselves unable to do their art work or pursue much loved hobbies when they're depressed. I'm certain, although I don't remember ever reading it anywhere, that depression and creativity are mutually exclusive. (Not madness and creativity. That's a different issue.) I'm talking about normal, mentally stable people who have bouts of both creativity and depression. When we are involved creatively, depression seems to recede. When we are depressed, those creative urges are nowhere to be found.

Depression and creativity
Are mutually exclusive!

Writing this book, doing this creative project, I find myself energized and not feeling depressed at all. I am, however, taking an anti-depressant medication every day. I told my primary care physician what I did for a career and that I was feeling overwhelmed, and he asked no questions. He just wrote out a prescription.

Every once in a while I'll decide I no longer need my anti-depressant. Fortunately I have a daughter-in-law who, after I've skipped the medication for less than a week, will say to me, "Are you still taking your Celexa? Because you have been cranky and short the last few days." Gee, I wonder if I really need it, don't you? That's one thing I've observed about anti-depressants. You won't be able to tell as much difference in your mood or well-being as will the people around you. You need a trusted family member or friend you can count on to monitor you and whose head you won't bite off if they report your increased edginess.

When you find yourself not caring as much about work, not feeling that your efforts are appreciated or worthwhile, that's a sign that you might be experiencing PTSD. Withdrawing from favorite activities, giving up an exercise program, for example, or not playing the piano when you usually play a couple times a week, these are all signs that should be taken seriously.

Clearly we all know that if we start thinking about that cold beer earlier and earlier in the day we need to pay attention. I've heard people who are suffering from PTSD also talk about not being aware of how much they're drinking or how many packs of cigarettes they're smoking. That's because one of the telling signs of posttraumatic stress is not being truly present for life. We live unconsciously when the conscious, real world becomes too much. This is a sign that it's time to make some life style changes.

Changes in behaviors, like more snacking, a craving for the oil and salt fast food provides, disrupted sleep or sleeping a lot more, shopping with a new vengeance or quitting the golf league you used to live for, are all warning signs. Any sort of isolating behavior and withdrawal from groups or family functions are signs of trouble. Now, let's be real. We all go through periods when we reorganize and reprioritize our lives. That's different. You can feel the difference from inside. The one you are controlling. The other is controlling you.

Last on the symptom list is falling for the physical self-improvement come-ons, which include anti-aging creams, new exercise equipment, the latest fad diet or any other type of the commercialism which suggests, "You're not okay the way you are. If you spend your money the way we want you to and buy what we're selling, you'll feel wonderful. Any profit we make from you is merely happenstance." Falling into this, whether it's as serious as cosmetic surgery or as negligible as some fancy new face cream, is another indicator of a trauma reaction. What this indicates is that you don't feel all right. Something needs to change. Why do we always start on the outside when this urge hits us? It never works. Camp out in a therapy waiting room sometime and check out all the beautiful, thin, cosmetically perfect women and all the buff, handsome fellows. Exterior perfection doth not a calm countenance produce.

Our Steps

Medicine is very helpful. Secondary PTSD, because it is less deep-seated than childhood or combat PTSD, seems to respond very well to anti-depressant medication, especially those medications with an anti-anxiety component. Your primary care physician or physician's assistant will be able to guide you to a medication which will take the edge off your edginess. If you had bronchitis or a sinus infection, surely less severe than pneumonia, you'd still take an antibiotic. Remember, it doesn't matter if the elephant is standing on your little toe or your whole foot, you are in trauma.

Therapy is very beneficial. Practice what we preach, eh? Quite a few practices offer a support group or a therapy group just for counselors. It would be common for a couple of therapists at a practice to form their own group based on similar ages or similar temperaments. They might meet once a month and talk about what's on their minds and what is heavy on their hearts, from personal matters to general practice issues. A great many therapists are also "in therapy" as the client.

Creativity is a sure-fire help with secondary PTSD. In one practice, for example, a practice of about twenty therapists, there are four artists, two gourmet cooks, a couple of great and devoted gardeners, an interior designer, a practitioner of energy work, a couple of writers, and that's just the women. The men practice, as do a number of the women, yoga, Tai Chi and martial arts. Almost all are walkers, from casual strollers to a marathoner. One of the men has horses and another has a small farm on a lake.

Many therapists also have spiritual practices. Mine consist of playing the piano, reading theology, and meditating. Colleagues have altars for meditation, spiritual groups to which they belong, religious affiliations, reading, and prayer rituals. It would be very difficult to do this work if one were without a faith background and felt life was transient and purposeless. Often it is only our faith, in the wide ranges of whatever faiths we possess, which compels us to labor on and trust that all things will be revealed in their own good time.

My Story

This whole book is, of course, my story. These case studies are a vital part of the pathway to my understanding of posttraumatic stress. I've said earlier in these pages and I want to repeat once more that I am not an expert on PTSD. These stories, signs, steps, tipping points, hypotheses and adages are what I've found and fashioned over the years to help me and those with whom I spend my days. If they are a help to you in any way, I am delighted. If they are not, I am sorry. Therapy is not one-size-fits-all. Different clients resonate with different therapists, and different therapists resonate with different therapeutic theories and techniques.

Even so, there are a few observations I would like to add before I end this story.

The first is to encourage you to use medicine if you or your doctor feels it is necessary or could be helpful. So many people believe anti-depressant medication to be "mind-altering" or "numbing." Nothing could be further from the truth. The medications used these days are SSRIs: selective serotonin re-uptake inhibitors.

In our brains are (among other things) serotonin, norepinephrine, and dopamine. Typically a doctor will first try to adjust a serotonin level. The SSRI mimics a natural function by keeping the serotonin in our brains. When we are under stress for as little as three weeks, our serotonin levels drop. And when we further anticipate stress, our bodies flush with and absorb the serotonin from our brains, emptying our brains of this "resiliency" chemical. Serotonin in our brains acts like shock absorbers in a car or insulation in a house. We are spared the worst jolts and the worst blasts--they are minimized by the protective layer of serotonin. An SSRI is a serotonin re-uptake inhibitor. It keeps the serotonin from being transferred into our bodies. It keeps the natural chemical in our brains. In effect, it closes the escape route.

Most psychiatrists say 85% of all the people who start taking an anti-depressant stop the medication too soon. Many experts estimate that most of the medications should be taken for two to five years. Some people might need such medication for the rest of their lives. If you live where there are distinct seasons and winters are colder and greyer, the only time to try going off anti-depressant medication is in the spring, when the days are growing longer and the sun is shining more brightly. That way we have nature on our side supporting our efforts.

What happens to us if we need anti-depressant medication and don't take it varies. Here's my metaphor of how it might be. Our brain is a glass bowl. We have water in the bowl, and the water is the serotonin in our brains. We float miniature marshmallows on the top of the water. These are the neurotransmitters in our brains. They need to talk to each other--to fire off each other and bump each other and communicate. Obviously, the more water (serotonin) in our bowl, the more the marshmallows (the neurotransmitters) will move.

The neurotransmitters move and this keeps a flow of ideas and thought processes moving in our minds. As the water level (serotonin) in our bowl lowers, which it will do whenever we are stressed, the marshmallows (neurotransmitters) get stuck on the side of the bowl. Our thoughts get stuck. Now I have never seen anyone's thoughts get stuck in a positive way, repeatedly saying, "I'm talented," or "I am a good person." No, instead our marshmallows always get stuck in the negative: "I wonder if he paid the mortgage. I bet he didn't pay the mortgage. That irresponsible moron is pushing us into bankruptcy. I bet there's a tag on the door. Does the sheriff come and make you leave everything in the house? What about my mother's silver?" The ideas are absolutely stuck on this negative run-away train of thought.

I remember working with a couple who really used this image to catch each other. He was on a rant during one of our sessions, and his wife finally punched him in the ribs and said, "Your marshmallows are stuck!" He was taken aback, but really it's difficult not to laugh or at least smile when someone says to you, "Your marshmallows are stuck."

Anti-depressants unstick your marshmallows by keeping a necessary level of water in the glass bowl. Try explaining that to a psychiatrist. Call me if they try to lock you up. I'll come keep you company.

A second generalization I want to mention is that our minds and our bodies are a unit. If you are having gastro-intestinal problems, by all means, see your physician. But remember that all the Prilosec in the universe isn't going to be effective if you keep thinking and believing and perceiving in ways which keep you in a constant state of stress. Likewise, if you are seeing a therapist to help with the stress, go to a physician and get the heartburn medicine, also. Anything which aids our bodies aids our minds, and anything which supports our mental health will strengthen our physical selves as well.

Many people come into therapy riddled with self-doubt because physicians have been unable to find the answers to ailments which are manifesting in their bodies. Pain, especially, can be such a difficult symptom to pin down. Mental issues like guilt and resentment and shame can show up as physical symptoms. Just because something manifests as a physical symptom doesn't mean it has only a physical cause, and just because something manifests as a mental health issue, anxiety, for example, doesn't mean there is only a mental cause. I defy you to have irritable bowel syndrome and not get anxious. For another example, mitral valve prolapse demonstrates the circularity of physical and mental health issues. The heart valve malfunction can cause fatigue, palpitations, chest pain and migraine headaches. This is what anxiety feels like, too. So, are you anxious because your heart is doing something weird or is your heart doing something weird because you're anxious? Sometimes, many times, the answer is both.

Third, therapists' offices and doctors' offices must be safe places where you can tell experiences which are humiliating and shameful. They must be. I have a client I've seen on and off for a number of years. She admits that sexual intercourse is painful for her, but she can't bring herself to tell her gynecologist. Some things are really embarrassing to talk about. So, write it down and hand the doctor a piece of paper. But find yourself a doctor and a therapist you can trust. Word of mouth and networking are great ways to hear about recommendations. Just remember, this person must be someone you can trust, not someone trusted by your friend or your aunt or the car mechanic. A "good" therapist or doctor is the one who is good for you.

Fourth, I fear I have made PTSD sound a lot like alcoholism: you'll always be in a state of recovery. Yes, I believe that to be true. However, alcoholics who stop drinking and work a program live fulfilling, serene lives and have fulfilling, secure relationships. Likewise, admitting and realizing that we are posttraumatic stress survivors will make a big difference in the quality of our remaining lives. We may never trust as easily as others and we may have to check ourselves for our own paranoias and prejudices, but is that so different from everyone else? We humans are an idiosyncratic lot. You may always have PTSD. I would say you would. The trick is transitioning from victim to survivor. The talent is in playing the cards we are dealt. The tipping point is often in reaching out to a trusted friend or a therapist and asking for some help.

Fifth, here are some general observations for every one of us, but even more essential for PTSD survivors:

Be kind to yourself.

Trust your own intuition and instincts.

Give your power away to no one.

Find blessings every day.

Give gratitude away.

Participate in only reciprocal relationships.

Learn to love silence and the beat of your own heart.

And lastly, PTSD is an explanation, not an excuse. It's up to you to make something positive out of everything that happens in your life, and PTSD is no exception. It is blatantly unfair that you are a posttraumatic stress victim. But you are a survivor. You're reading this book and I'm sure this is only one of the things you're doing to help yourself heal and be healthy. Keep it up. No one will do it for you. No one can. Only you can determine that this life you are living is going to be lived to the fullest and the richest and that no one--not a violent husband, not a voyeuristic brother, not a satanic mother, not a molesting father, not a sexually exploitative brother, not a neglectful mother, not an abandoning father, not an abusive, violent father, not a set of narcissistic, neglectful parents, not a sexually violating father, not a blaming mother, not combat, not drugs, not alcohol, not our temperaments, not adoption, not minority status, not a rapist, and not a life work which is challenging, draining and heart-breaking--nothing, nothing, nothing is going to keep you a victim when you can be a survivor. So, you have posttraumatic stress. What are you going to do about it?

■

List of Possible PTSD Indicators

Shoot yourself in the foot?

Anxiety out of nowhere?

Panic when nothing's wrong?

Mind never settles down?

Eating disorder? Overeat? Binge? Purge?

Diarrhea? IBS? Crohn's?

Fibromyalgia or chronic fatigue syndrome?

Feel different? Don't fit in?

Feel like you never belong?

Smoke to calm down?

Drink to forget?

Take drugs to numb?

Trouble trusting anyone?

Forget large segments of your childhood?

Mother who's critical and impossible to please?

Abusive or abandoning father?

Alcoholic parent?

Suicides in family?

Denied medical or dental care as a child?

Control issues as an adult?

Perfectionist?

Anal retentive or obsessive/compulsive?

Wish you were dead?

Find life meaningless?

Don't like to play or let your hair down or be silly?

Distrust your friends?

Have no friends?

Fractured family? People don't talk to others in the family?

No sex?

Can't get enough sex?

List of Possible PTSD Indicators

Dress to hide your body?

Dress to flaunt your body?

Hate your life?

Hate God?

Believe you're a loser?

Behave in passive/aggressive ways frequently?

Say "I don't know" a lot?

Experience gender confusion or sexual preference confusion?

Can't say "no"?

Can't make decisions?

This is a list of the most common descriptors therapists are likely to hear. It's based on twenty-two years of observation and experience. It's neither comprehensive nor conclusive. But if I heard you mention a number of these, I'd be aware of the possibilities of PTSD.

■

Notes to Therapists

It is not easy to work with posttraumatic stress survivors, especially when they're still in the victim stage. Most apparently, it's difficult because we have to hear about the   heartbreaking stress. I remember working with a client who stuttered. He was a successful executive of a big corporation. He recounted lying to his father at the age of four, and having his father toss him from his lap, yelling, "You are no longer a son of mine."   Fifty years later the pain was palpable and he cried.

In addition to being heartbreaking, therapy with posttraumatic stress survivors is faith testing. The stories of rape, molestation, torture and agony at the hands of usually a father, a kindly-looking grandpa, a "favorite" uncle, a "trusted" family friend, a cub scout leader, a youth group advisor, an older sibling's "polite" friends, this is bad enough, this profile of the perpetrator, but there is something even worse.

The perpetrator always has an accomplice: a silent mother, a deaf grandmother, an aunt who blindly looks the other way, a co-minister or scout leader or teacher who "suspects" but "doesn't want to make trouble" or "ruin anyone's reputation."

Let's assume that dad is the perpetrator. Then, most commonly, mom gives her silent consent. This is clearly and definitely not always true. But even if mom "doesn't know" and dad pulls it off single-handedly, still, in a child's mind, the mom who has warned, "I have eyes in the back of my head," "I can tell when you're lying," "Because I'm your mom and I said so," that mom didn't stop it. Let's look at the spiritual, emotional, intellectual and physical consequences.

Many spiritual teachers suggest that our "conceptualization of God" is limited by our conceptualization of our parents. If our parents are warm and loving, we can imagine a warm and loving God. If our parents are scorekeepers, hey, God has an accounting book and God is keeping track, and besides, if God sees everything (omniscient) and is always with us (omnipresent) and can do anything (omnipotent), then stopping dad (or whomever) from hurting us and helping mom (or whomever) see that it's happening should be no challenge at all for an omniscient, omnipresent, omnipotent One. Ergo, we have a deep and profound spiritual problem.

Notes to Therapists

Emotionally, children who are loved are loving. I'm sure you have read "If a Child" by Amanda Carter. You can find it on the internet by looking up her name or the name of the poem. Her eloquent point is that children become what they have endured. If they've grown up with hostility, she says, they learn to fight. If they've grown up with security, they learn to have faith. Children who grow up in negativity and pain become the hitters, the biters, the sluggers, the cutters, the head-bangers, the animal abusers, the fire-starters, and the vandals. Succinctly put, if you can't trust your own mother or father, who can you trust? And if you can't trust anyone, with whom can you connect? And if you can't connect with anyone? It gets cold and lonely in the solitary confinement of a wounded heart.

Intellectually, school is going to bring out two extremes: why bother, or school is their only triumph. In the "why bother" category, we have to realize that kids who are being abused are likely to be depressed, anxious, reclusive, non-engaging children. To make matters worse, these children are likely to act different, look different, be standoffish or hostile and perhaps even appear retarded. These are not the children who get praised and attended to in school either by teachers or other students. Having never been loved, or at least not consistently, these are not very loveable children.

The second extreme of intellectual consequences at school would seem to be preferable: school is where they shine. Many trauma surviving kids with average or better intellectual abilities are likely to opt for achievement because it brings validation and affirmation. The downside is that the school triumph is frequently unbalanced by any other development. So, we have spiritually and emotionally stunted children who are "smart." These are the geeks, the nerds, the loners in the corners, eyes downcast, eating their cheese sandwiches alone, staying in chemistry labs after school. Learning to make pipe bombs? Because you see, they are only smart, not wise. These children have no spiritual or emotional template for their knowledge.

Physically, you've seen them and they are obvious. They are "too." They are the teenaged girls who dress like sluts or nuns.

They are the teenaged boys who are pierced and tatooed. They may wear black, but their hair is orange or purple. They might look at you, but they are more likely to look through you or to ignore you. They are different and they are defensive. Even someone who says hello to them is suspect. "Why are you saying hello? What do you want?"

If you are a therapist who works with children, you see these things. If you are a therapist who works with adults, you see adults at different levels of adult functioning who are pedaling furiously uphill, trying to compensate for childhoods and adolescences which cemented into their minds and hearts the lessons of exclusion and isolation. Scared children, like frightened kittens, will frequently scratch and snarl no matter the size of the body they're in or the various functioning and coping mechanisms they've learned.

So, fellow therapists, leave your ego at the door when you enter your office. Find a support group and use it. Pay attention to yourself and your own system of warning signs which indicate you are overwhelmed and need to re-balance and re-prioritize your life. Remember that if you don't put on your own oxygen mask first, you can't be sure of being around to help anyone else with theirs. And play.

I recommend grandchildren, especially young ones. I have one with whom I watch Elmo, one with whom I build train tracks of great and daring complexity, and one with whom I play school and tell stories. If you don't have any handy that you can play with, find some. They remind me, as they will you, that we come into the world with innocence and a hungry capacity for loving and being loved. If this innate ability is de-railed, we can and must get it back on track, both for ourselves and for those with whom we spend our days. It's inside each of us, this ability to laugh and smile and enjoy each other. We may have to sift through layers of wackiness and sludge, but it's there and it can be found. Just dig. Dig as deeply and as gently and as respectfully as possible. But dig, and don't stop digging, until you find the buried treasure of the wholeness with which we each entered life. Didn't you always want to be an archeologist?

Other Books by Susan Rau Stocker

Naked Courage
By Susan Ross

As a victim assistance advocate, Sara Miller devotes her working life to aiding victims of heinous acts. As much as she knows about trauma and survival, nothing has prepared her to become the victim. She is simply driving home from work one day, daydreaming about how happy she is with her new life, when she sees a woman stranded by the side of the road. She decides to stop and help. Life as she knows it ends with that decision. Sara, the social worker who tirelessly leads victims back to sanity, is swamped in a nightmare more evil and depraved than any she has ever encountered. And she finds herself alone in her terror, left to find her own way home.

Heart
By Susan Ross

It began one passionate evening. It had to end one bittersweet weekend. For Ruth was leaving for the grandeur of Italy and the career of her dreams. And Tom could never leave his caring wife and the son who needed him so completely. So Ruth and Tom parted, perhaps never to touch again. But though they could no longer be together, they shared a love more enduring than the ocean that separated them. A love more desperate than the tragedies they both had to face. And though Ruth and Tom tried to avoid it, though they knew they could not change the courses of their lives, something was drawing them together. Some undeniable longing burning deep within their hearts.

See www.SusanStocker.com for other books
by Susan Rau Stocker.